KING LEAR IN OUR TIME

KING LEAR
IN OUR TIME

By Maynard Mack

University of California Press 1972
Berkeley and Los Angeles

UNIVERSITY OF CALIFORNIA PRESS
BERKELEY AND LOS ANGELES, CALIFORNIA
© *1965 by The Regents of the University of California*

FIRST PAPERBACK EDITION 1972
ISBN: 0-520-02157-6

LIBRARY OF CONGRESS CATALOG CARD NUMBER 65-23949
DESIGNED BY JANE HART
PRINTED IN THE UNITED STATES OF AMERICA

For F. B. M.

SINE QUA NON

Acknowledgments

The substance of this essay was delivered in the form of three lectures before members of the Department of English of the University of California at Berkeley during my tenure of the Beckman visiting professorship, September to January, 1964-5. I take this occasion to record my gratitude and also that of my wife for the unfailing kindness shown us by all members of that distinguished department throughout our stay, and for their courtesy and patience especially on the evenings of the thirtieth of November and the seventh and fourteenth of December.

I am aware that the content of the essay also owes much to others. Apart from specific obligations recorded in the notes and the pervasive debt that every essay on a play of Shakespeare's owes to its predecessors, I wish to register particular thanks to the members of a graduate seminar, who, during the academic year 1963-4, when some of the directions of this undertaking were being meditated, supplied information, challenge, stimulus, and a valuable variety of views. I am further grateful to my former student, Evelyn Goldman Hooven, who has understood better than most what it means, in Keats's words, to "burn through"

>   the fierce dispute
>   Betwixt Damnation and impassion'd clay;

and to Marvin Frederick Edell, on whose unpublished doctoral dissertation (Yale School of Drama, 1959), entitled "Lear in

Acknowledgments

London: A Survey of Interpretations of the Role on the London Stage from Richard Burbage to Charles Laughton," I have drawn at several points in my first chapter. To my friend and colleague, Eugene M. Waith, I am indebted for scrutinizing parts of the manuscript with his usual charitable rigor.

The quotation from "On Cutting Shakespeare" by Bernard Shaw is reprinted with the permission of The Public Trustee and the Society of Authors.

An earlier version of chapter 3 was published by the *Yale Review* (LIV [Winter, 1963–1964], 161–186) under the title " 'We Came Crying Hither': An Essay on Some Characteristics of *King Lear*." Copyright by Yale University.

MAYNARD MACK

London
20 April 1965

Contents

CHAPTER ONE

Actors and Redactors

That Shakespear is a bore and even an absurdity to people who cannot listen to blank verse and enjoy it as musicians listen to an opera (Shakespear's methods are extremely like Verdi's); that Mr. George Robey, heroically trying to find jokes crude enough for an audience of rustic Tommies, would shrink from Touchstone's story about the beef and the mustard; that we who think it funny to call a man's head his nut remain joyless when Shakespear calls it his costard (not knowing that costard is an apple); that Benedick cannot amuse or fascinate the young ladies who have adored Robert Loraine and Granville-Barker as Jack Tanner; that William's puns are as dead as Tom Hood's or Farnie's; that Elizabethan English is a half-dead language and Euphuist English unintelligible and intolerable: all these undeniable facts are reasons for not performing Shakespear's plays at all, but not reasons for breaking them up and trying to jerry-build modern plays with them, as the Romans broke up the Coliseum to build hovels. . . . The simple thing to do with a Shakespear play is to perform it. The alternative is to let it alone. If Shakespear made a mess of it, it is not likely that Smith or Robinson will succeed where he failed.

BERNARD SHAW

1

K*ing Lear* is a problem. Lamb, as everyone knows, judged the role of the king unactable.[1] Thackeray found the play in performance "a bore," despite his feeling that "it is almost blasphemy to say that a play of Shakespear's is bad."[2] Tolstoi deplored "the completely false 'effects' of Lear running about the heath, his conversation with the Fool and all these impossible disguises, failures to recognize and accumulated deaths."[3] And Bradley, who regarded the play as Shakespeare's greatest work but "too huge for the stage," drew up a long list of gross "improbabilities" that no one has succeeded in arguing away.[4]

Among the grosser improbabilities that Bradley points out are Edgar's and Kent's continuing in disguise well after the purposes of disguise have been served; Gloucester's willingness to believe, when Edmund shows him the forged letter, that one son would write to another when both are living in

---

[1] "On the Tragedies of Shakespeare" (1808), *The Life, Letters, and Writings of Charles Lamb*, ed. Percy Fitzgerald (n.d.), IV, 205.

[2] *The Letters and Private Papers of William Makepeace Thackeray*, ed. Gordon Ray (1945), II, 292.

[3] L. N. Tolstoi, "On Shakespeare and the Drama," tr. V. Tchertkoff, *Fortnightly Review* (N.S.), LXXXVII (1907), 66.

[4] A. C. Bradley, *Lectures on Shakespearean Tragedy* (1904), pp. 247, 256 ff.

the same house, and specifically would put in writing such patricidal meditations as these; Gloucester's failure to show surprise when suddenly, during the fight with Oswald, his escort drops into peasant dialect; Gloucester's determination to go to Dover to commit suicide, as if there were no other way or place of dying; and finally, Edmund's long delay in telling of his order on the lives of Lear and Cordelia after he himself is mortally wounded and has nothing to gain. One could add considerably to the list. Probably we should add to it at least the unlikely nature of Edgar's disguise, the implausibility that neither his disguise nor Kent's is seen through, the fact that Gloucester is blinded for his treason instead of being killed, and the "almost babyish" goings on, as one reviewer describes them, of the play's first scenes:

The old man who parcels out his kingdom by the map; the daughters who overdo their thanks with a fulsome excess that any child would see through; the simple, obvious contrast of the daughter who cannot say "thank you" at all; the absurd wrath of the old man over a situation that any father with any daughter could not fail to understand. Then follow undignified things, acts of schoolboy rudeness, pushings and kickings and trippings up. . . . How, you ask, are these primitive, rather absurd, folks going to excite in you the proper tragic emotions? [5]

It will not do to say that these things go unnoticed in performance. What we notice in performance is whatever we bring with us a capacity to notice, and this includes all we have learned from reading and discussion. Moreover, anyone who goes to a performance of *King Lear* with his eyes open will soon be aware that what he watches onstage deviates markedly from the ordinary Shakespearean norms of proba-

---

[5] A. B. Walkley, *The Times* (London), 1909; reprinted in *The English Dramatic Critics*, ed. James Agate (1932), p. 270.

bility in tragedy. In this play alone among the tragedies we are asked to take seriously literal disguises that deceive. Romeo's appearing masked at the Capulet ball and Iago's advising Roderigo to "defeat thy favor with a false beard" in following Desdemona to Cyprus (a circumstance we never hear of again) obviously put no similar strain on credulity. This is the only Shakespearean tragedy, too, in which a number of the characters are conceived in terms of unmitigated goodness and badness, and the only one, apart from the early *Titus*, where the plot is made up of incidents each more incredible — naturalistically — than the last: from the old king's love test and Kent's return to serve him as Caius, through Edmund's successful rise, Edgar's implausible disguise, Lear's mad frolic in the storm with beggar and fool, to Gloucester's leap and Edmund's duel with a nameless challenger who subsequently proves to be his brother. This is the heady brew of romance, not tragedy. If Polonius had seen a performance of *King Lear*, we can be sure he would have invented a suitable compound name for its kind: something like "tragical-comical-historical-pastoral-romantical," each of which terms might be defended as suiting one aspect of the play.

Neither will it do to pretend that the problematic *King Lear* is an invention of the scholar and literary critic. Quite the reverse. All that is necessary to appreciate the puzzles the play poses onstage is to think seriously about producing it. Mr. Peter Brook, we are told, described it, while readying it for his recent production with Paul Scofield in the title role, as "a mountain whose summit had never been reached," the way up strewn with the shattered bodies of earlier visitors — "Olivier here, Laughton there: it's frightening." [6] Miss Mar-

---

[6] As quoted by Charles Marowitz, Brook's associate in the production, in "*Lear* Log," *Encore*, X (1963), 22.

garet Webster, whose experience in directing Shakespeare
for all sorts of actors and audiences is formidable, has called
King Lear "the least actable of the four plays" (i.e., *Hamlet,
Othello, King Lear,* and *Macbeth*), adding that "*Macbeth,*
whatever the spiritual or abstract significance with which it
has been variously endowed, has always been played for its
tremendous dramatic impact," and that "*Othello* insures a
sweep of movement which, in the theatre, overwhelms all
theoretical debate as to the motivation of its principal characters" — whereas in *Lear* "the lack of this fundamental theatre
economy" makes difficulty.[7] Reviewers and theatre critics
have many times voiced similar reservations. When friendly
to the play, they have questioned at the very least whether
it is possible to perform the first storm scene (III,ii) "so that
it looks and sounds like an intelligible piece of theatre."[8]
When unfriendly, they have been more pungent:

You like Shakespeare?
Maybe this is an unfair question, because there is an awful
lot of Shakespeare, and you could be pardoned for liking some
but not all.
Frankly, that's the way I feel. I have never liked "King Lear,"
the excessively wordy and expensive bijou which opened at the
National Theatre last night with Louis Calhern in the lead
role . . .
Mr. Calhern munches on most of the scenery and, at one junc-
ture, nearly gnaws the occupants of the first row center, but that
is the requirement of the title part and he plays it to what used
to be called the hilt.
If you will harken back to the days of your childhood when
somebody made you read it, you will recall that the story con-

---

[7] *Shakespeare Today* (1957), p. 214.
[8] Brooks Atkinson, *New York Times,* Dec. 26, 1950, reviewing the Louis
Calhern–John Housman production.

6

cerns the mad convolutions of this King and the deceitful behavior of his three daughters and their separate swains. Things
get so tough, as you'll remember, that the monarch flips his
skimmer.[9]

Give or take a Broadway cliché or two, this approximates
many a theatregoer's impression of *King Lear* today, onstage as well as off, and (if the truth were told) many a student reader's.

If *King Lear* as a work of literature is either Shakespeare's
greatest achievement, freely compared by its devotees to the
sublimest inventions of the artistic imagination, or else a
work of childish absurdity inspiring "aversion and weariness" [10] in others besides Tolstoi; if as a play it is either
unsuited to actual stage performing, or on the contrary is
only understood when performance has tied together the
"series of intellectual strands" which compose it [11] and drawn
our attention "away from what otherwise might seem puz-
zling, distasteful, or foolish," [12] clearly we have a problem.
My aim in the following pages is to throw whatever light
I may on the scope and nature of that problem by coming at
the play from three historical directions. The first chapter will
consider some aspects of its stage history, since, actable or
not, *King Lear* has a long line of famous performances behind it in which great actors have been thought to distinguish
themselves and by which audiences have believed themselves edified and moved. The second chapter will shift to
the genetic pole and consider the play's sources, meaning by
that term not so much the Lear legend, or the Gloucester

---

[9] John McLain, *New York Journal-American*, Dec. 26, 1950.

[10] Tolstoi, *op. cit.*, *Fortnightly Review* (N.S.), LXXXVI (1906), 981.

[11] Brook's opinion, as quoted by Marowitz, *op. cit.*, p. 21.

[12] Arnold Szyfman, "*King Lear* on the Stage: A Producer's Reflections,"
Shakespeare Survey, XIII (1960), 71.

plot that Shakespeare found in Sidney, as the traditions of thought and feeling in terms of which he shaped his materials. These traditions were, we have reason to believe, intelligible to his contemporaries with an immediacy that in our theatre requires enormous effort to recapture. Finally, like all Shakespeareans who are allowed access to paper or even a whitewashed wall, I shall seize the opportunity in the third chapter to sketch out my own notions of what in the play speaks most immediately to us, who live four centuries after its author's birth.

II

The stage history of *King Lear* has been haunted, possibly from its very beginnings, by practical problems of communication with the audience. We do not know why the mad scene in the "farmhouse," where Lear stages a mock trial of his hard-hearted elder daughters with joint stools to represent them (III,vi), is missing from the folio text, printed seventeen years after the play was first acted. The excision may have been made only to shorten the playing time; but it may also have been made, as Professor Kenneth Muir acknowledges in his Arden edition,[13] because the original audiences laughed. If we may judge from the asides that Edgar utters to guide the spectators' response to Lear's antics whenever he is on the stage with him, this possibility was a matter of real concern to the playwright, who knew, as the creator of Malvolio and Hamlet well might, that for the most part contemporary audiences expected madness to be entertaining. One other complete scene missing from the folio text is that in which Kent and a Gentleman

---

[13] Introduction, p. xlviii.

discuss Cordelia's reception of the news of her father's sufferings (IV,iii). Here they wrap Cordelia in a mantle of emblematic speech that is usually lost on a modern audience's ear and difficult for a modern actor to speak with conviction. We cannot assume that the Elizabethan actor and audience had our kinds of difficulty with the scene, but what kind did they have — or was this omission too intended merely to shorten the performance?

During the first seventy-five years of its existence, we can make only guesses like these about the history of *King Lear* onstage. We know that on the reopening of the theatres after the Restoration it continued to be played for a time "as Mr. Shakespeare wrote it, before it was altered by Mr. Tate" — so John Downes assures us in his *Roscius Anglicanus* (1708)[14] — but we do not know what interpretation it was given or what success it met. There may, however, be an answer to the latter question in the fact that the play was before long wholly rewritten by Nahum Tate, so that between 1681, the date of Tate's redaction, and 1838, the year in which Macready restored almost the whole of Shakespeare's original text in a historic production at Covent Garden, Shakespeare's *King Lear* was never, as far as is known, seen in performance. Tate's *King Lear* occupied the stage and throve.

Tate's *King Lear* invites ridicule and deserves it, but is nonetheless illuminating. A line in its verse prologue may be taken to mean (what would not be at all surprising) that Shakespeare's version had ceased to appeal to Restoration playgoers, whose favored diet, apart from comedy, consisted mainly of heroic plays and other subspecies of epic romance. "Why should," Tate writes,

---

[14] P. 26.

9

These Scenes lie hid, in which we find
What may at once divert and teach the Mind?

From his dedicatory letter it is clear that he regards his bringing of Shakespeare's scenes before the Restoration public as a pious tribute. He has been emboldened to it by a persuasive friend (a certain Thomas Boteler) and by his own "Zeal for all the Remains of Shakespeare." When we open to the text, we discover that his zeal for these remains has carried him to invent a love affair between Cordelia and Edgar, to omit France and Lear's Fool, to give Cordelia a waiting woman named Arante, to supply a happy ending, and to omit, conflate, and rearrange Shakespeare's scenes while re-writing (and reassigning) a good deal of his blank verse. Tate's own description of these efforts, in his letter to Boteler, suggests that, like "art" in Aristotelian aesthetics, his function has been to help extravagant "Nature" — "a Heap of Jewels, unstrung, and unpolish'd; . . . dazling in their Disorder" — realize its implicit goals. And in a curious literal-minded way, that is exactly what he has done. He has seized on the romance characteristics of Shakespeare's play and re-stored it to what must have seemed to him its intended genre.

In his version Cordelia is abducted by ruffians at the command of Edmund, who intends to rape her. The ruffians are driven off by Edgar in his Poor Tom disguise — upon which, he reveals himself and receives avowal of his beloved's affection. They *exeunt* together with a convenient flint and steel ("the Implements Of Wand'ring Lunaticks") to light a fire at which she can dry her "Storm drench'd Garments." In similar vein, we have a scene in "*A Grotto*" with "Edmund *and* Regan *amorously seated, listening to Musick*"; a scene in which Edmund receives and reads a billet-doux from each of Cordelia's sisters; an episode in which Gloucester repines at his incapacity to take part in the battle, comparing himself (in a reminiscence of Job) to a "disabled Courser" who snuffs the fighting from afar and foams "with Rage"; and another episode in which King Lear, asleep in prison with his head in Cordelia's lap, rouses as Edmund's soldiers enter to hang Cordelia, and holds them at bay, killing two of them, till Edgar and Albany come to his rescue. Tate had an unerring eye for romantic melodrama, and his handling of his original points up very clearly for all who are willing to see them the melodramatic potentialities of the plot from which Shakespeare began.

The other goal of Tate's changes was to clarify motivations. He notes in his dedicatory letter that the virtue of the love affair he has invented for Edgar and Cordelia lies in rendering "Cordelia's Indifference, and her Father's Passion in the first Scene, probable," and in giving "Countenance to Edgar's Disguise, making that a generous Design that was before a poor Shift to save his life." What this means, in detail, is that Tate's Cordelia consciously tempts her father to leave her dowerless in order that Burgundy may refuse her (Tate's play, as noted, omits the King of France altogether), and that Tate's Edgar, whom after her own rejection Cordelia unexpectedly rejects that she may test his devotion, determines to disguise himself (rather than make away with himself in his lover's despair) on the chance that he may yet be of service to her. With the same end in view, Tate firms up the appearances of plausibility throughout. His play opens with Edmund's soliloquy, in order that Edmund may inform us that he has incensed his father against his brother, with

A Tale so plausible, so boldly utter'd,
And heightned by such lucky Accident,

That now the slightest Circumstance confirms him,
And base-born *Edmund* spight of Law inherits.

Here Edmund is credited with an initial deception of his father offstage and earlier, details remaining unspecified, in order to render more credible the scene in which Gloucester accepts the forged letter. Lear's scene of folly is also prepared for. Immediately following Edmund's soliloquy, Gloucester and Kent enter to him, and when he has been introduced by Gloucester as the "generous Boy" whose loyalty he means to reward, both men deplore the forthcoming division of the kingdom, bearing witness in advance to Lear's "Infirmity" of age, his customary "wild Starts of Passion," and his "Temper . . . ever . . . unfixt, chol'rick and sudden."

Other difficulties are met with similar expedients. Edmund's deception of his brother takes place while Edgar is in a brown study induced by Cordelia's rejection of his love and hardly follows what his brother says. Cornwall's speech marking Edmund for his own — "Natures of such deep trust we shall much need" — is given by Tate to Regan and extended by a comment which prepares the audience for their subsequent liaison. Gloucester's incriminating letter "guessingly set down" and sent by "one that's of a neutral heart And not from one oppos'd" becomes in Tate some despatches Gloucester has himself addressed to the Duke of Cambrai urging help against the sisters, and thus gives Cornwall a more acceptable motive for his cruelty to the old man. When Edgar is seen with his blind father, he tells us immediately why he does not reveal himself: it is for fear the old man's heart will break of extremes of grief and joy. Such is Tate's method throughout. The upshot of his reworking is that there is no longer question but that the play is indeed tragical-comical-historical-pastoral romance and, in a sad, shriveled way, effective "theatre." And so it proved for one hundred and fifty-seven years.

III

I have dwelt on Tate's *King Lear* because its stage history is actually longer than any other continuous stage history the play has yet had, and because it established, I think, for a very long time (even after the text had been restored) the performer's approach to the play. Tate's text was the vehicle for all the actors who tried Lear during Pope's and Johnson's century: Betterton, George Powell, Robert Wilkes, Barton Booth, Anthony Boheme, James Quin, Garrick, Spranger Barry, John Kemble, and several more. We know very little about any of them before Garrick. Lear was widely reputed to be Garrick's finest role. His interpretation of the part, as well as the sensibility of his period, may be seen in Edward Tighe's account of his effect on the Montgomery sisters:

The expression of the eldest was wonderful and such as the mighty master would have smiled to see. She gazed, she panted, she grew pale, then again the blood rose in her cheeks, she was elevated, she almost started out of her seat, and *tears began to flow*.[15]

Garrick played the king as an "honest, well-meaning, ill-used old man," [16] partly perhaps because his own stature was unsuited to a more majestic mien, but largely, one suspects, because that was the one genuine human thing that Tate's *King Lear* had left in it. A contemporary describes him in the role

---

[15] *Private Correspondence of David Garrick*, ed. James Boaden (1831), I, 157.

[16] Thomas Wilkes, *A General View of the Stage* (1759), p. 241.

as a "little old white-haired man . . . with spindle-shanks, a tottering gait, and great shoes upon the little feet";[17] and though this was intended to ridicule him, there is no reason to doubt its substantial accuracy. We know from other sources that great age was emphasized in his make-up, that his performance colored "all the Passions, with a certain Feebleness suitable to the Age of the King,"[18] and that in his own view, expressed in a letter to his friend Tighe, "*Lear* is certainly a *Weak* man, it is part of his Character — violent, old and *weakly* fond of his Daughters."[19] What Garrick saw in the play as a whole, according to Professor G. W. Stone, who had studied Garrick's production of *King Lear* more carefully than any man alive, was a "Shakespearean play which could surpass competition from all writers of pathetic tragedy and could command the emotional pleasure of tears more successfully than sentimental comedy."[20]

Garrick was a very great actor and played the play that he saw in *King Lear* with a kind of absolute distinction, if we may judge from the lyrical responses of his contemporaries. But he was the prisoner of the Tate text and perhaps of his audiences' expectations. After toying at one point with the idea of restoring the Fool, he abandoned the idea as too "bold an attempt,"[21] and though urged early in his career

---

[17] Sir John Hill, *The Actor, or A Treatise on the Art of Playing* (1755), p. 151.

[18] [Samuel Foote], *A Treatise of the Passions* (1747), p. 22.

[19] *Letters of David Garrick*, ed. D. M. Little and G. M. Kahrl (1963), II, 682.

[20] See his "Garrick's Production of *King Lear*: A Study in the Temper of the Eighteenth-Century Mind," *Studies in Philology*, XLV (1948), 91. See also A. C. Sprague, *Shakespearean Players and Performances* (1953), pp. 21–40, and *Shakespeare and the Actors* (1944), pp. 281–297, and K. A. Burnim, *David Garrick, Director* (1961), pp. 141–151.

[21] Thomas Davies, *Dramatic Miscellanies* (1783), II, 267.

to put away Tate and give *"Lear* in the *Original, Fool* and all," [22] he never got further than restoring part of the original Shakespearean verse: the story remained "Tatefied," including love affair, happy ending, and all. With respect to his audience's expectations, Garrick's caution was well advised. We know how Samuel Johnson felt about the death of Cordelia ("I was many years ago so shocked by Cordelia's death that I know not whether I ever endured to read again the last scenes of the play till I undertook to revise them as an editor"), [23] and when George Colman produced a version of the play in 1768 with the love story omitted and (it would seem) the catastrophe restored, it received short shrift. One review observed: "[Colman having] considerably heightened the distress of the catastrophe, we doubt very much whether humanity will give him her voice in preference to Tate"; [24] and another:

We have only to observe here, that Mr. *Colman* has made several very judicious alterations, at the same time that we think his having restored the original distressed catastrophe is a circumstance not greatly in favour of humanity or delicacy of feeling, since it is now rather too shocking to be borne; and the rejecting the Episode of the loves of Edgar and Cordelia, so happily conceived by Tate, has beyond all doubt, greatly weakened the Piece, both in the perusal and representation . . .[25]

----

[22] *An Examen of the New Comedy, Call'd The Suspicious Husband, With Some Observations upon Our Dramatick Poetry and Authors, To Which Is Added, a Word of Advice to Mr. G-rr-ck* (1747), p. 35.

[23] "General Observations" on *King Lear* in his edition of Shakespeare (1765), reprinted in *Samuel Johnson on Shakespeare,* ed. W. K. Wimsatt, Jr. (1960), p. 98.

[24] *The Theatrical Review, or The New Companion to the Playhouse* (1772), I, 213

[25] *Ibid.,* p. 334. In his *Shakespeare from Betterton to Irving* (1920) G. C. D. Odell assigns this quotation — I believe erroneously — to *The Theatrical*

Even Colman had not ventured so far as to restore the Fool. "After the most serious consideration," he tells us in his Advertisement to the published copy, "I was convinced that such a scene 'would sink into burlesque' in the representation and would not be endured on the modern stage." [26]

For all the talent of the eighteenth-century actors, there was nothing in their representations of Lear to give the lie to Lamb's penetrating summary: "Tate has put his hook in the nostrils of this Leviathan, for Garrick and his followers, the showmen of the scene, to draw the mighty beast about more easily." [27]

IV

The qualities in *King Lear* which impressed the eighteenth century, when it confronted Shakespeare's play instead of Tate's, may be gathered from Samuel Johnson:

The tragedy of *Lear* is deservedly celebrated among the dramas of Shakespeare. There is perhaps no play which keeps the attention so strongly fixed; which so much agitates our passions and interests our curiosity. The artful involutions of distinct interests, the striking opposition of contrary characters, the sudden changes of fortune, and the quick succession of events, fill the mind with a perpetual tumult of indignation, pity, and hope. There is no scene which does not contribute to the aggravation of the distress or conduct of the action, and scarce a line which does not conduce to the progress of the scene. So powerful is the

---

Register, or *A Complete List of Every Performance at the Different Theatres, for the Year 1769*, a publication I have not been able to identify.

[26] *The History of King Lear, As It Is Performed at the Theatre Royal in Covent Garden* (1768), p. v. This published version retains Tate's ending.

[27] *Op. cit.*, IV, 206.

current of the poet's imagination that the mind which once ventures within it is hurried irresistibly along.[28]

When we place beside this a passage from Hazlitt's review of Edmund Kean's production of 1820, we realize at once that the critical emphasis has significantly changed:

There is something . . . in the gigantic, outspread sorrows of Lear, that seems to elude his grasp, and baffle his attempts at comprehension. . . . [The passion in Lear is] like a sea, swelling, chafing, raging, without bound, without hope, without beacon, or anchor. Torn from the hold of his affections and fixed purposes, he floats a mighty wreck in the wide world of sorrows. . . . Abandoned of fortune, of nature, of reason, and without any energy of purpose, or power of action left, — with the grounds of all hope and comfort failing under it, — but sustained, reared to a majestic height out of the yawning abyss, . . . [the character of Lear] stands a proud monument, in the gap of nature, over barbarous cruelty and filial ingratitude. . . . There are pieces of ancient granite that turn the edge of any modern chisel: so perhaps the genius of no living actor can be expected to cope with Lear. Mr. Kean chipped off a bit of the character here and there: but he did not pierce the solid substance, nor move the entire mass.[29]

"Gigantic, outspread," "like a sea," "a mighty wreck," "reared to a majestic height out of the yawning abyss," "ancient granite," "mass"— all this is a new world, and it does not stem exclusively from Hazlitt's characteristic intellectual abandon and hyperbole of style. Lamb's testimony, we recall, is essentially the same: "they might more easily propose to personate the Satan of Milton upon a stage, or one of Michael

---

[28] *Op. cit.*, p. 96.
[29] *The London Magazine*, I (1820), 687.

Angelo's terrible figures." [30] And the note continues to be heard right down the century to Bradley, whose lectures bring the Romantic expansionist interpretation of Shakespeare to a noble close:

the immense scope of the work; the mass and variety of intense experience which it contains; the interpenetration of sublime imagination . . . ; the vastness of the convulsion both of nature and of human passion . . . the strange atmosphere, cold and dark, [enfolding the play's figures] and magnifying their dim outlines like a winter mist; the half-realized suggestions of vast universal powers working in the world of individual fates and passions. [31]

The theatre, however, is more conservative than are literary critics. There is very little evidence to show that any of the great nineteenth-century productions of *King Lear* departed essentially from the lines laid down by Garrick's feeble and downtrodden king. Edmund Kean played for passion rather than pathos, and was scolded by the *Examiner* for doing so: "[Lear's] ebullitions of rage cannot be more freely given than by Mr. Kean, but there is something in that gifted Actor, which is at war with a delineation of corporeal and mental weakness; and consequently of the pathos which may spring out of them." [32] Yet even Kean missed the grandeur of the part sadly, as Hazlitt testifies. His madness was "imbecility instead of phrenzy"; [33] "he drivelled and looked vacant." [34]

Macready also played *King Lear* for passion, but not to the

---

[30] *Op. cit.*, IV, 205.

[31] *Op. cit.*, p. 247.

[32] *The Examiner* (London), Mar. 2, 1823.

[33] *The Courier* (London), Apr. 25, 1820.

[34] *The London Magazine*, I, 689.

exclusion of pathos, especially in his relations with the Fool. In Macready's production of 1838 the part of the Fool was restored to the play for the first time since the seventeenth century, together with a text that was now entirely Shakespearean apart from some cuts and rearrangements.[35] Macready had even graver doubts than Garrick's and Colman's about how the Fool would go down with a contemporary audience, and considered omitting the part till after rehearsals were under way. But on describing to a colleague his notion of "the sort of fragile, hectic, beautiful-faced, half-idiot-looking boy that he should be," it was observed to him that the part should be played by a woman, and this suggestion won him over.[36] We can see here very clearly that the processes of sentimentalizing set in motion by Tate did not come to a halt when Tate's text was replaced. The Restoration and eighteenth century had excluded the Fool as coarse and grotesque; the Victorian period readmitted him, but not as a cracked brain guarding "incommunicable secrets" — this is Robert Speaight's fine phrase;[37] rather, as a sort of feverish Peter Pan, or a Burne-Jones rendering of Matthew Arnold on Shelley.

Macready's conception of the role of Lear suggests that possibly he had encountered Lamb's strictures on the usual Lear of the theatre ("an old man tottering about the stage with a walking stick"), or Hazlitt's on Kean. "The towering range of thought with which [Lear's] mind dilates, identify-

---

[35] Kean, in 1823, had replaced much of Tate's fifth act, including the happy ending, and had been criticized by reviewers for not extending his restorations to the whole.

[36] *Diaries of William Charles Macready*, ed. William Toynbee (1912), I, 438.

[37] "The Actability of *King Lear*: Reminiscences of Thirty Years of Performances," *Drama Survey*, II (1962), 51.

ıng the heavens themselves with his griefs," Macready noted, "and the power of conceiving such vast imaginings, would seem incompatible with a tottering trembling frame."[38] But as with Macready's Fool, so with his King. He was moving in his tragic kingliness and paternity; he spoke the first curse with a terrifying "still intensity,"[39] the second with a "screaming vehemence" that "greatly exceeded in power the first,"[40] and, like all his predecessors, drew "sighs and tears which shook the audience" when he woke to recognize Cordelia.[41] But nothing in the reviews suggests that he brought to life, or was in any way aware of, the brooding, mythic, almost apocalyptic hints and intimations that for most of us today lie just beyond the story of domestic pathos and seem already to be glimpsed fitfully in the sentences of Hazlitt and Lamb, quoted earlier, and in Coleridge's superb outburst on III,iv:

O what a world's convention of agonies is here! All external nature in a storm, all moral nature convulsed, — the real madness of Lear, the feigned madness of Edgar, the babbling of the Fool, the desperate fidelity of Kent. Surely such a scene was never conceived before or since! Take it but as a picture for the eye only, it is more terrific than any which a Michel Angelo, inspired by a Dante, could have conceived, and which none but a Michel Angelo could have executed.[42]

Though Macready was an exceptionally fine actor, like

---

[38] *Macready's Reminiscences and Selections from His Diaries and Letters*, ed. Sir Frederick Pollock (1875), I, 207.

[39] *The Examiner*, Feb. 4, 1838.

[40] William Winter, *Shakespeare on the Stage* (1915), p. 401. See also Lady Juliet Pollock, *Macready as I Knew Him* (1884), p. 104.

[41] Winter, *op. cit.*, p. 402.

[42] *Lectures and Notes on Shakespeare . . . Now First Collected by T. Ashe* (1908), p. 341.

Garrick, and like Garrick one of very few of the older actors who could feel his way to a total conception of a role rather than play a pastiche of electrifying moments in the manner of Kean, he remained the prisoner of conceptions that had got their start with Tate. So did the remainder of the nineteenth century. The role of Lear was altogether sentimentalized by Phelps; played by Booth, according to one review, like "an angry, conventional Polonius," [43] and according to Tennyson, in a way "most interesting, most touching and powerful, but not a bit like Lear"; [44] and then "degraded" by Irving ("to the level of a doddering lunatic") [45] in a performance after which one drama critic is reported to have said to his colleagues: "Now who's going to tell the truth about this?" [46] To sum up with the verdict of a witty student of mine, [47] himself a promising actor, the Lears of the nineteenth century after Macready may "best be pictured as a halting procession of senile old men, trudging at various rates of speed toward the sacred grove of Bathos."

V

Two changes by Kean's and Macready's time "revised" the impression of *King Lear* onstage almost as thoroughly as Tate had done. One was the use of stage machines. Already in Kean's production of 1820 there had been provided for the heath scenes a river over-

---

[43] *Bell's Life in London, and Sporting Chronicle*, Feb. 19, 1881.

[44] Reported by Winter, *op. cit.*, p. 449.

[45] H. B Baker, *A History of the London Stage and Its Famous Players, 1576–1903* (1904), p 305.

[46] See Laurence Irving, *Henry Irving, the Actor and His World* (1951), p. 551.

[47] Donald D. Knight, formerly of the Yale School of Drama.

flowing its banks and "scenic trees . . . composed of distinct boughs which undulated in the wind, each leaf . . . a separate pendant rustling with the expressive sound of nature itself." [48] When Macready produced his wholly Shakespearean *King Lear* in 1838, such effects were continued and improved. "From beginning to end," said the reviewer for *John Bull*:

the scenery of the piece . . . corresponds with the period, and with the circumstances of the text. The castles are heavy, sombre, solid; their halls adorned with trophies of the chase and instruments of war; druid circles rise in spectral loneliness out of the heath, and the "dreadful pother" of the elements is kept up with a verisimilitude which beggars all that we have hitherto seen attempted. Forked lightnings, now vividly illumine the broad horizon, now faintly coruscating in small and serpent folds, play in the distance; the sheeted element sweeps over the foreground, and then leaves it in pitchy darkness; and wind and rain howl and rush in "tyranny of the open night." [49]

The persistence of this taste in staging *Lear* through the rest of the century may be best gauged from the comment of G. C. D. Odell, to whose pioneering *Shakespeare from Betterton to Irving* all studies of Shakespeare in performance are necessarily in debt. It was the opinion of Odell, writing as late as 1920, that this passage from *John Bull* describes an ideal performance — "a nobly conceived and ably executed revival of a great tragedy; in intention nothing could surpass it even to-day." [50]

---

[48] George Raymond, *Memoirs of Robert William Elliston, Comedian* (Concluding Series, 1845), pp. 232–233.

[49] *John Bull*, Jan. 28, 1838 (XVIII, 45).

[50] *Shakespeare from Betterton to Irving*, II, 211.

The other theatrical change that shielded nineteenth-century audiences from the savage impact of the play as Shakespeare wrote it was localization in time. Those who have *King Lear* fresh in mind will recall that the primitivism of its atmosphere and the folk-tale cast of the "choosing" episode in the first scene are offset continually by a vivid contemporaneous Elizabethanism, giving the effect, as so often in Shakespeare, of no single time and therefore all time. No member of Shakespeare's original audience, hearing Edgar's chatter on the life of farm communities (III,iv) or Lear's on urban knavery (IV,vi), or looking at the symbolic hierarchies of state and family in their "robes and furr'd gowns"(I,i), could doubt for a moment that the play was about a world with which he was deeply and centrally engaged. Such engagement by Victoria's time was a commodity not easily to be enjoyed.

We must be careful not to exaggerate the impairments suffered by Shakespearean drama when replacement of the apron stage by curtain and proscenium increased the imaginative distance between spectator and action; or when elaboration of scenery and scene changing and stage machines impinged on the role that Shakespeare had assigned to poetry, sometimes rendering it superfluous, sometimes swallowing it up in noise (as happened invariably with the storm scene in *Lear*), and always so far extending the playing time as to require cutting the poetic text severely. We must not exaggerate the losses, but some loss there certainly was, increased in the case of *Lear* by the sentimentalization which was a legacy from Tate. When to these factors was added the archaeological impulse of the nineteenth-century stage to convert poetry and myth into history, something like a dead end was in sight for all plays like *King Lear* in which poetry and myth contribute most of what rises above the level of *drame bourgeois.*

It made little difference which historical epoch was chosen: Macready played the play with druid circles, Charles Kean as belonging to "the Anglo-Saxon era of the eighth century," [51] Irving as of "a time, shortly after the departure of the Romans, when the Britons would naturally inhabit the houses [that the Romans had] left vacant." [52] The result was to mask the play's archetypal character, distancing its cruelties as the errors of a barbarous age with no compelling relation to oneself. This attitude the abrupt opening scene too easily encourages in any case. It so encouraged it in Samuel Johnson that he temporarily lost his usual sensitivity to what is *semper, ubique, et ab omnibus*:

Perhaps if we turn our thoughts upon the barbarity and ignorance of the age to which this story is referred, it will appear not so unlikely as while we estimate Lear's manners by our own. Such preference of one daughter to another, or resignation of dominion on such conditions, would be yet credible if told of a petty prince of Guinea or Madagascar.[53]

And it continued to encourage opinion of this kind for a century and a half. Here is the reaction of a London theatre critic in 1909:

The people remind you of some simple South Sea Islanders in some 18th century traveller's narrative — peering through the wrong end of a telescope, expressing their emotions by uncouth

---

[51] Charles Kean's preface to his acting edition, quoted by Odell, *op. cit.*, II, 352. Garrick had introduced historical costuming — "Old English Dresses" — in his last production of the play, May 21, 1776 (*The London Chronicle*, May 21–23, 1776).

[52] *The Times* (London), Nov. 11, 1892.

[53] In his "General Observation," *op. cit.*, p. 96.

dances, and filled with delight by the present of some coloured beads.[54]

VI

The eighteenth-century *King Lears* with their benign ending were perhaps the natural product of an age which held that under the appearances of things lay an order of justice which it was the job of literature to imitate, not to hide. Those of the nineteenth-century, in which Shakespeare's text had been increasingly restored but was trammeled in stage effects and historical place and time, gave equally natural expression to the principles of a period whose best poet (happily he did not often practice his own preachment) said that poetry was made of the real language of real men, and whose most systematic critic imagined he had engaged what was important about literature when he talked of *race, milieu, moment.*

In a number of ways, our own century seems better qualified to communicate and respond to the full range of experience in *King Lear* than any previous time, save possibly Shakespeare's own. We are familiar with the virtues of the bare unlocalized Elizabethan platform stage, and can recover them at will, with the immense added resource of modern lighting. After two world wars and Auschwitz, our sensibility is significantly more in touch than our grandparents' was with the play's jagged violence, its sadism, madness, and processional of deaths, its wild blends of levity and horror, selfishness and selflessness, and the anguish of its closing scene. We have not the Victorians' difficulty, today, in discerning behind its foreground story of a family quarrel inti-

---

[54] A. B. Walkley, *The Times*, Sept. 4, 1909. (Walkley goes on to show, however, that the play gets "hold of you" in spite of this.)

mations of mortality on a far grander scale: we know that we go to see in Lear one who is as much a portent as a man [55] — "a great oak struck by lightning," [56] "a stricken Colossus," [57] a "broken column at whose feet others bewail their lesser woes," [58] a figure out of "Blake, with a suggestion of Durer" [59] — and that the play as a whole, with its kings, beggars, fools, blindness, madness, and storm, casts shadows of unearthly grandeur on any twentieth-century imagination that will submit itself to it. Its fascination for us is plain from the statistics of performance. During the eighteenth century there were nineteen distinct productions on the London stage, five by Garrick; during the nineteenth century, twenty-one, fourteen by 1845, but only six in the sixty-two years from 1858 to 1920. Already (to 1962) in this century there have been twenty-three London (and I include Stratford-on-Avon) productions, nineteen beginning with 1931, or better than one each biennium through the past three decades. As a critic for the London *Times* wrote in reviewing Olivier's performance in 1946, it has been "a period rich in notable Lears." [60]

Rich indeed. Without going outside the English stage or the period since 1930, one may name John Gielgud, William Devlin, Randall Ayrton, Donald Wolfit, Laurence Olivier,

---

[55] Granville-Barker's description of the Lear of I,i: "more a magnificent portent than a man." *Prefaces to Shakespeare* (1952), I, 285.

[56] Richard Buckle, reviewing John Gielgud's 1955 production of *King Lear*, in *The Observer* (London), July 31, 1955.

[57] *The Times*, Jan. 26, 1943, in a review of a performance by Donald Wolfit.

[58] James Agate, reviewing John Gielgud's first production, in *The Sunday Times* (London), Apr. 19, 1931.

[59] *The Times*, in the review above mentioned of Donald Wolfit's performance.

[60] Issue of Sept. 25, 1946.

Stephen Murray, Michael Redgrave, Charles Laughton, Paul Scofield. Some of these have taken the part in as many as four separate productions,[61] and all have played it with gratifying and instructive differences. Interpretations have ranged from Gielgud's monarch of "Olympian grandeur" [62] in 1940 (from all accounts the greatest performance of our time) — through Olivier's "Swell-head the Tyrant" of 1946, an interpretation containing, we are told, "an illuminating remnant of the fussy, feeble, Justice Shallow" [63] — through Redgrave's towering ruin of 1953, who even in the opening scene was "almost too decrepit to draw his huge sword" [64] — to Laughton's uncompromising repudiation of the "grand" Lear in 1959, in favor of an intense portrayal of a smaller, more immediately sympathetic figure, less king than father, less father than "representative of the common man," [65] whose physical appearance is said to have reminded specta- tors of "Father Christmas" and "Old King Cole." [66]

Interpretations of the play as a whole have also run the gamut. The stress of Byam Shaw's production in 1959 for Laughton was "modern," "realistic," "human" — calculated "to put the play within the scope and comprehension of a mass Shakespearean audience." [67] The Louis Casson-Gran- ville Barker production of 1940 for Gielgud appears to have been largely based on Barker's intuition of "megalithic gran-

---

[61] Gielgud in 1931, 1940, 1950, 1955; Wolfit in 1943, 1944, 1945, and 1953.

[62] *The Times*, Apr. 16, 1940.

[63] Ivor Brown, in *The Observer*, Sept. 29, 1946.

[64] *The Times*, July 15, 1953.

[65] *The Times*, Aug. 19, 1959.

[66] E.g., W. A. Darlington (*New York Times*, Sept. 13, 1959) and Muriel St. Clare Byrne ("*King Lear* at Stratford-on-Avon, 1959," *Shakespeare Quarterly*, XI [1960], 191).

[67] *Ibid.*, pp. 190, 205.

deur" in the play as in the monarch.[68] Gielgud's 1955 production, with contributions by the Japanese designer Isamu
Noguchi, sought a setting and costumes which "would be
free of historical and decorative conventions, so that the
timeless, universal, and mythical quality of the story may be
clear" [69] — though the effect proved at odds with the intent
and, as Gielgud recalled later, "little short of disastrous." [70]
In 1962, Peter Brook tried for a "frame of reference" as
"Beckettian" as possible, and a "world . . . like Beckett's
. . . in a constant state of decomposition," even down to costumes of leather "textured to suggest long and hard wear"
and furniture "once sturdy, but now decaying back into its
hard, brown grain." [71] A year earlier (to cross abruptly an
ocean and a continent) Herbert Blau of the San Francisco
Actor's Workshop had mounted the play with a group of
Method actors by relating it for them to Beckett and Genêt.[72]

All this is healthy, no doubt, and shows the vitality of the
play as well as of the twentieth-century theatre. But the
question as to whether it is Shakespeare's play that is com-
municated by these means is not settled by the presence of
enthusiastic audiences and rave reviews (even supposing,
which is far from the truth, that most of these productions
drew such audiences and reviews): Garrick's Tatefied and
sentimentalized text also drew them, and so did Macready's
coruscating lightning and leaves. If I may consult my own

---

[68] *Op. cit.*, I, 271. Gielgud's notes on Barker's hints, set down at the time
in his rehearsal copy, may be consulted in his *Stage Directions* (1963), Ap-
pendix I.

[69] Program note (quoted in *The Times*, July 27, 1955).

[70] "A Shakespearean Speaks His Mind," *Theatre Arts*, XLIII (1959),
69–71.

[71] Marowitz, *op. cit.*, p. 21.

[72] See his "A Subtext Based on Nothing," *Tulane Drama Review*, VIII
(1963), 122 ff. The quotations below are reprinted by permission.

experience during the same three decades, I am obliged to register the suspicion that our stage, for all its advantages, and with a few honorable exceptions, has worked out ways of altering the effect of Shakespeare's text which are quite as misleading as any our ancestors used, and seem to spring, at least in large part, from the same determination to rationalize, or generalize, or unify according to a particular plan what is not regular, not rational, or not really unifiable on that plan.

VII

The siren's rock on which efforts to bring *King Lear* to the stage (as well as, in some quarters, critical efforts to interpret it) oftenest split is the desire to motivate the bizarre actions that Shakespeare's play calls for in some "reasonable" way. This desire lay behind many of Tate's alterations, as we saw. It helped influence the nineteenth century to rationalize absurdity and barbarity by attributing them (in the manner exemplified by Dr. Johnson's allusion to petty princes of Madagascar) to some appropriately remote and barbarous time or place. It prompted Bradley to regard his considerable list of inconsistencies and implausibilities as serious "dramatic defects." And it seems to have misled Mr. Empson, usually an astute critic, into seeing in Lear's speeches to Gloucester in Dover fields a sex interest that is "ridiculous and sordid" in so elderly a man [73] — as indeed it may have to be considered if we assume that the relation of Lear to his speeches is the same as that of (say) Hedda Gabler to hers.

Such expectancies have disposed most directors and actors in our period to ignore Shakespeare's clear signposts (in-

---

[73] William Empson, *The Structure of Complex Words* (1951), p. 138.

forming us that psychological structure is not what we are to look for) in favor of rationalistic expedients of varying absurdity. Laughton's "funny old Father Christmas in a white nightgown, mild and chubby, looking forward to a party where he is to give away the presents," [74] was, among other things, a way of supplying character-motivation to Lear's perplexing behavior in the opening scene, as was Gielgud's senile mandarin of 1955, "all mutterings, shakings, graspings, and palsied twichings." [75] But these solutions were purchased at high cost to the "great image of authority" — inviolable, charismatic, a kind of *primum mobile* (as the monarch always is in the Renaissance) of the political and social macrocosm, and properly too its chief stay against anarchy. This is the Lear which Shakespeare's opening scene calls for and without which both the subsequent collapse of the image and the anarchy generated by its removal lose force. Something like a climax in this rationalizing mode was reached in Peter Brook's production for Paul Scofield in 1962. There in I,iv, evidently to justify Goneril's complaints about her father's retinue and thus motivate her insolence to him, Lear's knights literally demolished the set, throwing plates and tankards, upending the heavy table on which presumably the king's dinner was soon to be served, and behaving in general like boors [76] — as if the visible courtesy of

[74] Darlington, *loc. cit.*

[75] Richard Buckle, in *The Observer*, July 31, 1955.

[76] "Scofield is a Stalin . . . a guttural upstart whose behavior is so arbitrary and graceless, so jack-booted and ham-fisted, that audiences may begin by sharing the shocked embarrassment of his family and in-laws. . . . This Lear wolfs his food, hammers the table while he cackles at dirty jokes, and overturns the table in fury when crossed. He even belches in the middle of his farewell to his daughter. . . . And so another aspect of Lear is erased. As well as the King, we have lost the High Priest." Alan Brien, "Openings:

their spokesman earlier (I,iv,54-78), Albany's significant unawareness of what Goneril is complaining about, and Lear's explicit description of his knights:

> My train are men of choice and rarest parts,
> That all particulars of duty know,
> And in the most exact regard support
> The worships of their name —

had no existence in the play.

Lear is not an easy domestic guest: this we know from his conduct in the first scene, and from however much we may choose to believe of the list of grievances his daughter catalogues to Oswald in I,iii. But to justify Goneril is to obscure from the audience the relentless movement by which the man who is cynically humored so long as (in the Fool's words) he bears bags is maneuvered into surrender by two daughters whom Kent calls "dog-hearted," Albany calls "Tigers, not daughters," and the gentlest voice in the play calls "Shame of ladies!" This movement begins to take shape in I,i ("We must do something and i' th' heat"); is implemented, with Oswald as tool, in I,iii ("Put on what weary negligence you please, . . . I'd have it come to question"); is reported on and perhaps expanded in the letters Goneril sends Regan, which decide the latter to be absent from her house when Lear arrives there; and is finally revealed, in II,iv, as a visible trap, between whose ponderous jaws, whether by studied plan or opportunism, Lear is first squeezed dry of all his remaining dignities and illusions and then spat away.

The destruction of Goneril's dining hall by Lear and his

London," *Theatre Arts*, XLVII (1963), 58. It is fair to add that Brien found the losses compensated by "the man of flesh and blood." Many others including myself looked in vain for such a man.

knights was so vivid an act of aggression in the Brook production that it fixed Lear in the mind as not only a vindictive but a powerfully supported figure, who might easily take back his gift of the kingdom at any time and was silly not to. It also obscured the fact that in the play's terms, Lear being her father, nothing can possibly justify Goneril. As Lear feels that Cordelia in scene i "wrench'd" his "frame of nature From the fix'd place"—an image which invites us to see beyond it the ruining of a great building or even a rupture in the cosmic frame itself—so Goneril's actions are eventually seen by Albany to be violences striking at the very foundation of the natural order. On the one hand, she is like the flood which "cannot be border'd certain in itself," and will, given the opportunity, as Ulysses says in *Troilus and Cressida*, "make a sop of all this solid globe"; on the other hand, she is like the branch that tears itself from the fostering tree. Throughout the play, Shakespeare brilliantly humanizes both Goneril and Regan by the shifting passions and appetites he traces in their speech, but this is a different matter from "motivation." The motivation of the sisters lies not in what Lear has done to them, but in what they are. The fact that they are paradigms of evil rather than (or as well as) exasperated spoilt children whose patience has been exhausted gives them their stature and dramatic force.

VIII

The newest and most unpromising form that efforts to rationalize *King Lear* have taken is that of playing what is called in today's theatrical jargon the "subtext." A play's subtext, according to the views of those who favor this approach, is the underlying "reality" to which its verbal text points: "language is gesture, there is a life to which the words give life, and it is to that life we

[are] finally responsible." [77] As a device for training actors, I am willing to believe that this conception has merit. It derives from but extends familiar Stanislavsky techniques which seek to help the actor transform the disjunct speeches and gestures of an acting part as written into some sort of organic and, as it were, psychosomatic continuum. But in the hands of many directors in today's theatre, where the director is a small god, subtext easily becomes a substitute for text and a license for total directorial subjectivity — in ways that may readily be illustrated from the recent productions of Peter Brook and Herbert Blau.

The most obvious result of subtextualizing is that director and (possibly) actor are encouraged to assume the same level of authority as the author. The sound notion that there is a life to which the words give life can with very little stretching be made to mean that the words the author set down are themselves simply a search for the true play, which the director must intuit in, through, and under them. Once he has done so, the words become to a degree expendable. This view of a text probably does no harm when applied to plays whose destiny is to be consumed this season and forgotten next. In these, directors and actors often collaborate throughout rehearsals and trial run, and the resulting "vehicle," as it is so rightly called, conveys the talents of both.

Directing a classical text might, one supposes, be conducted on more modest principles. And in theory it is. Modern directors of Shakespeare, no less than Garrick, profess to love him. As Blau points out in his interesting and sensitive account of his San Francisco production, "We have done some plays in which we have thrown a text to the winds of our own psychological behavior — but who is going to feel

---

[77] See below, p. 34.

superior to *King Lear*?" [78] A page earlier, in a description of Blau's management of the heath scene, we meet with this:

Let me say this: we lost words. To do what we tried to do, especially on the heath, and make every word absolutely intelligible is almost impossible. There was an incredible amount of detailed activity, incessant motion — what we were after was the muscular projection of the interior nature of madness. I am not saying that every word shouldn't be intelligible; but I don't think it was the fault of the actors' methodology . . . so much as what was required of them. Nor am I saying that the scenes were unintelligible. Far from that. Whatever they didn't have, one felt the storm as a nightmare; one saw the descent to absolute dispossession on the part of the King; one felt the visceral dominance of lunacy in that lucid trial of the daughters. To the extent that the words are the life of the design, we did everything we could to respect them. Even our improvisations were not improvisations emancipated from the text; but language is gesture, there is a life to which the words give life, and it is to that life we were finally responsible. But let me emphasize again: we relinquished clarity only in those marginal cases where what was being done couldn't be done without relinquishing it — given those circumstances and those actors.

In short, even in *King Lear*, when the chips are down for the subtextualist, rather than relinquish "what we were after," or "what was being done" by directoral inspiration, he will relinquish the author's text.

And what *was* being done on this occasion? How marginal were the situations in which clarity had to be relinquished? We may gather an answer from Blau's description of the staging of the storm. It is worth attention because it shows the often very fine creative imagination by which, in the

---

[78] *Op. cit.*, p. 131.

modern directorial theatre, Shakespeare's own imaginative effort, his text, is swallowed up. "The unifying factor" in the storm scene, says Mr. Blau, "was the music, chaos dazzled by its own coherence." The phrase alone might give us pause: how will a mere actor make out where chaos itself is dazzled? But we hasten on to discover how the bedazzlement was achieved:

It was an electronic score. . . . The basic sound was a kind of drone of vast amplitude . . . composed . . . of three elements: the sound of Lear's voice saying the word "I" into an open piano; a single pure pitch; and a cello note — which was a subliminal factor, buried in the storm, but which emerged as the storm progressed as an impulse of healing. That cello note later emerged in the sleep music of Lear, in the reunion with Cordelia. Exquisite, lovely then. But in the storm it was part of the swell of derangement. The three elemental sounds were impacted on tape, improvised upon, made dense until the drone appeared, like the troubled breathing of the earth projected by Lear upon the universe. Over this was imposed another sound track of accidental electronic sounds; during the whole sequence, perhaps about thirty-five minutes, during which the sound never stopped, these occurred at unpredictable moments. Thus, the scene could never be the same. They came whirling or hissing or singing out of the atmosphere, and the actors had to play with them. Then there was still another sequence of sounds, orchestrated explicitly with Lear's "Blow winds" speech — in which the synchronization of language, sound, and action was meant to establish a perfect harmony of derangement, Lear and the storm locked by sound in a kind of cosmic embrace. Some of the sounds were fierce, indescribably active; and the Fool danced half-witted in their ambience, like an hallucinated lightning bug.

. . . Tom screamed. The Fool screamed. Lear screamed. Adding the unison of their derangement to the sound and fury of the storm. This unison was what we worked for. In the body.

They moved like animals, improvising on each other's gestures and sounds, borrowing them from each other, virtually changing identities. A metamorphosis. A sound would screech down from above; Tom would seem to pluck it out of the air; Lear would move as if he had created it. The Fool would slither between them, recovering the cloak which Lear had given Tom, jealous that his function was being preëmpted. Synesthesia. We worked for a precise disorder of sense impressions. . . .[79]

Some of the ideas here are fascinating. They would be superbly at home in *King Lear* rewritten as a tragic ballet. But the homely circumstance that the reader of this hypnotic account must not lose sight of is that, onstage for thirty-five minutes during the heath scenes, three sequences of electronic sounds — some "fierce, indescribably active," one sequence a complete variable occurring "at unpredictable moments," all the sequences overlaid by wild screams and accompanied by "incessant motion . . . the muscular projection of the interior nature of madness" — competed for the spectator's attention with Shakespeare's words. We may safely guess which factor won. But this, I suspect, was not the only or perhaps the chief damage. Shakespeare's words were intended, with the help of a few rumblings of cannon balls in the Elizabethan theatre's upper storey, to produce a storm in the audience's imagination. When instead the storm is produced *for* the audience with such brillance of detail by nontextual means, Shakespeare's text is left without a function, and so is the audience's imagination. The spectator

---

[79] *Ibid.*, pp. 128–129. Blau's somewhat different account of his production in *Theatre Arts*, XLV (1961), 80, may suggest that certain of the effects described above existed more fully in the producer's retrospective imagination than in the audience's experience at the time. Several spectators have assured me that they were quite unaware of these intentions.

understands the storm in the sense or senses the director has attached to it; he is not compelled, as he is by Shakespeare's poetry, to grope for meanings and relations and to compound them for himself.

IX

This point becomes clear if we consider a further aspect of the Brook and Blau productions. Mr. Blau's subtext was, he tells us, based on Nothing — that is to say on the "nothing" uttered by Cordelia in her first answer to her father's question, and in his reply: "Nothing will come of nothing." Following this lead, the San Francisco production presented in Edgar's disguising an effort to feel "what it is like *to become nothing*," in Lear's madness the upsurge of "Nothing," in Goneril's and Regan's stripping away of Lear's knights a "rhythm of reduction, back to Nothing;" in Cordelia's "no cause, no cause" the mystery of what issues from Nothing — her *acte gratuit* of I,i, and later her gratuitous charity. Even the exit of the three madmen from the heath was contrived on a "movement . . . with a regressive motion, as if Lear were thinking back to that elusive Nothing." [80]

One is impelled again to pay tribute to the subtlety of the director's imagination. Once more, however, to the extent that any of his intention managed to cross the footlights as meaning, directorial imagination has run away with the play. Shakespeare's text unquestionably includes the arabesque on Nothing that Blau notes, together with many cognate allusions of the same character; but in the play itself all these must struggle for *lebensraum* with other allusions and patterns of widely different colorings and contrasting implica-

---

[80] *Ibid.*, pp. 122–129.

tions. They are not extrapolated out, as here, to suffuse the whole with one hue. How subjective and simplistic the view of *King Lear* is that finally emerges from this kind of reading may be assessed from Blau's comment on suicide, "In this world," he writes, "we are back, as the Bishop says in [Genêt's] *The Balcony*, in the sacred clearing where suicide at last becomes possible. In fact, the subtext constantly brings the characters to that question which Gloucester makes explicit and which Camus thought the major philosophical question of our time: why not suicide?" [81]

This is intoxicating stuff — but what resemblance does it bear to the play that Shakespeare wrote? One casts about in vain to name the characters that the play "constantly brings" to the question of suicide. Gloucester? Yes, but only once. Lear? Not a trace of it. Edgar? Only to thwart his father's intent, and in his mad speeches as the unjust serving-man on the heath. Cordelia, Kent, Albany, the Fool? Unimaginable. Not really imaginable for Edmund or Cornwall either. Only Goneril in the play actually commits suicide, and her act, undertaken to avoid retribution for her poisoning of Regan and her plot on her husband's life, is hardly what Genêt and Camus had in mind.

According to Charles Marowitz's "log" of the Brook production, for which he was assistant director, the search for the subtext of *King Lear* in London yielded equally exhilarating results. "Everywhere one looks," he notes, summarizing Brook's conception of the play and presumably his own,

one sees only the facade and emblems of a world, and, ironically, as characters acquire sight, it enables them to see only into a void. . . . It is not so much Shakespeare in the style of Beckett

---

[81] *Ibid.*, p. 124.

as it is Beckett in the style of Shakespeare, for Brook believes that the cue for Beckett's bleakness was given by the merciless *King Lear*.[82]

Merciless, it may be. Yet Marowitz confesses that it took tinkering to give the play the bleakness that Beckett is supposed to have derived from it. "One problem with *Lear*," he notes, in a sentence that seems to contemplate the problem as the driver of a bulldozer contemplates a tree, "is that like all great tragedies it produces a catharsis. The audience leaves the play shaken but assured." Clearly this would not do in a production of *King Lear* describable as "Beckett in the style of Shakespeare." Something had to be done, "and i' th' heat."

Accordingly, "to remove the tint of sympathy usually found at the end of the Blinding Scene,"

Brook cut Cornwall's servants and their commiseration of Gloucester's fate. Once the second "vile jelly" had been thumbed out of his head, Gloucester is covered with a tattered rag and shoved off in the direction of Dover. Servants clearing the stage collide with the confused blind man and rudely shove him aside. As he is groping about pathetically, the house-lights come up — the action continuing in full light for several seconds afterwards. If this works, it should jar the audience into a new kind of adjustment to Gloucester and his tragedy. The house-lights remove all possibility of aesthetic shelter, and the act of blinding is seen in a colder light than would be possible otherwise.[83]

At the end of the play, where "the threat of a reassuring catharsis is even greater," Marowitz suggested that

instead of silence and repose, which follows the last couplet, it might be disturbing to suggest another storm — a greater storm

---

[82] *Op. cit.*, p. 21.
[83] *Ibid.*, pp. 28–29.

—was on the way. Once the final lines have been spoken, the thunder could clamour greater than ever before, implying that the worst was yet to come. Brook seconded the idea, but instead of an overpowering storm, preferred a faint, dull rumbling which would suggest something more ominous and less explicit.[84]

X

After such knowledge, what forgiveness—for those who would be content to see *King Lear* as Shakespeare wrote it? To censure virtuosity and experiment seems ungenerous: no one good custom must be allowed to corrupt the world. To insist on fidelity to ancient texts may be pedantic: it is the scholar's habit at his least endearing. Yet the question that inevitably arises in the mind after studying either of these recent treatments of *King Lear* (or indeed, most we have been given in my lifetime) is Robert Frost's question: what to make of a diminished thing? However liberating the conception of subtext may be in theory, it is reductive in practice, as has been the directorial theatre generally.[85] Both are too likely to persuade to "nameless somethings" (as Pope calls unformed creative impulses in his great lines on literary distortion in the *Dunciad*) in preference to the author's text; both encourage emphasizing a part of the text in lieu of the whole and amplifying that part so as to unmake the intricacies and overset the balance of the

---

[84] *Ibid.*, p. 29.

[85] One of the more spectacular current instances of directorial reductiveness was Marowitz's *Hamlet*, performed at the Akademie der Künste in West Berlin on Jan. 20, 1965. An hour in length, the play had lost several of its characters, including Horatio; lines given in the original to one speaker had been reassigned to another; the part of the prince was played in white clownface. My point is not that such experiments are wrong, only that they diminish Shakespeare along with our opportunities of seeing what Shakespeare actually wrote.

original; even in the most sensitive hands, their effect is to do the work that in poetic drama is properly the work of the audience's imagination, and thus make "entertainment" out of what should be participation in a ritual enactment of one's own deepest experience; and this is to say nothing of the cuttings, rearrangements, and reapportionings which are also justified in their name.

It is true that Shakespeare's play, with a little adjusting, can be made to yield Brook, Blau, and Beckett as it was formerly made to yield Tate and Garrick. Like the spokesman of *Leaves of Grass* it is large, it contains multitudes; and it is inexhaustibly patient of the images of ourselves we thrust upon it, including the image I am about to thrust upon it in these pages. What is also true is that our extrapolations from it in order to get a hook into the nostrils of Leviathan do no permanent harm. The mountain remains, as Brook says, long after those who seek to climb it have been decently interred. Does this mean that nothing like the whole play is actable, that the best we can do in the theatre, as so often in our criticism, is to capture one dimension of it at a time? Or does it mean that something like the whole play might be actable and knowable if we were to come to it with other ends in view than rationalizing the irrational, regularizing the irregular, and unifying on a particular plan what cannot be unified on such a plan? These are the questions to which I now turn.

CHAPTER TWO

Archetype, Parable, and Vision

> In no other of the plays, I think,
> unless it be *Macbeth*, are we so conscious . . . of a vision of
> things to which the action itself is but a foreground.
>
> HARLEY GRANVILLE-BARKER

*I*t is well known to Shake-
speareans, though probably not to most theatre audiences,
that Shakespeare may have been moved to write *King Lear*
by an occurrence in real life. He had long been acquainted
with Lear's story, we may assume, since it is told in a number
of books with which he was familiar: Holinshed's *Chronicles*,
A Mirror for Magistrates, *The Faerie Queene*, and others,
while the outlines of the Gloucester plot had been laid down
in Sidney's chapter on the Paphlagonian king in another
book in which he sometimes read, *The Countess of Pem-
broke's Arcadia*. Yet it is possible that the Lear story was
brought to life in Shakespeare's mind by the experience of a
contemporary, Sir Brian Annesley. Annesley, a gentleman
pensioner to Queen Elizabeth, had three daughters, the two
elder married; the youngest, unmarried, was named Cordell. In late 1603, a year or two before the composition of
Shakespeare's play, Annesley's eldest daughter and her husband seem to have taken steps to have him declared incompe-
tent, and to lay hands on his possessions. Cordell resisted the
move, persuaded Sir Robert Cecil by a letter that her father
deserved a better reward for his services to the late Queen
"than at his last gasp to be recorded and registered a Luna-

tic," and succeeded in sequestering his estate even when, on his death soon after, the eldest daughter contested the will.[1] Though nothing can be proved, nothing is easier to imagine than that, when news of these events was bandied about London, the youngest daughter's name, not to mention other resemblances, reminded gossipers of the story of King Lear — which besides being well known from the works earlier mentioned, had been acted at the Rose in the mid-nineties.[2] Hence the legendary story could conceivably have been thrust to the

---

[1] On this, see C. C. Stopes, *The Third Earl of Southampton* (1922), p. 274; G. M. Young, *Today and Yesterday* (1948), pp. 300–301; Kenneth Muir's Introduction to the Arden edition of *King Lear*, p. xlviii*n*; and, for the documents, *Historical Manuscripts Commission: Salisbury MSS.*, XV (1930), 262, 266.

The incident is not easy to reconstruct. The sisters' married names were Lady Grace Wildgoose and Lady Christian Sandys, but there is no mention of the latter's participating in the proceedings against Annesley. Lady Wildgoose, the elder, and her husband seem to have initiated the case, Wildgoose, Timothy Law, and Samuel Lennard representing to Cecil on Oct. 18, 1603, that they had visited Annesley as Cecil (apparently in response to their overtures) had authorized them to do, and that they had found him "altogether unfit to govern himself or his estate." On Oct. 23, Thomas Walsingham, James Crofts, and Lennard, instructed by Cecil to take inventory, reported to him that they had done so, and had sealed up Annesley's chests "and other things of value," but that in view of "the present emulation between the two gentlewomen" (Lady Wildgoose and Cordell) for "the government of his person," a determination of guardianship would have to be made by Cecil. It was at this point that Cordell intervened, asking that custody of her father be bestowed on Sir James Crofts, "who out of the love he bare unto him in his more happier days, and for the good he wisheth unto us his children, is contented upon entreaty to undergo the burden and care of him and his estate without intendment to make any one penny benefit to himself . . . as also to prevent any record of Lunacy that may be procured hereafter."

[2] See E. K. Chambers, *William Shakespeare* (1930), I, 469–470; W. W. Greg, "The Date of *King Lear* and Shakespeare's Use of Earlier Versions of the Story," *The Library: Transactions of the Bibliographical Society*, XX (1940), 377 ff.

fore in Shakespeare's consciousness by the modern instance, or the modern instance could have reached his ear with the legendary story attached; even if it did not, the association would have been an easy one for a literary mind to make.

The possibility that actuality shared with fiction in the genesis of *King Lear* seems to me appealing — not for any influence we may safely assess from that quarter, but as symbol and prefiguration of the effect the play has produced on readers and audiences through the years: as a strange, powerful, yet sometimes uneasy union of high-flown parable and vision with a homely verisimilitude such as Shakespeare was never to surpass. Whether or not Lamb was right about the actability of the role of Lear, his sense of the profound dualism in the part and the play was sound. We do have before us, not only onstage, as he argued, but in the study too, "an old man tottering about . . . with a walking stick, turned out of doors by his daughter on a rainy night" — a type of the discarded parent whose atavisms will appear, male and female, in a thousand nineteenth-century tear-jerkers and twentieth-century soap operas, a man all too human who smells very much of mortality, and in whom the slow erosion of dignity and strength by age, fatigue, and heartbreak is traced by a great artist with a fine — happily pre-Freudian — naturalism:

> No, you unnatural hags,
> I will have such revenges on you both
> That all the world shall — I will do such things,
> What they are, yet I know not, but they shall be
> The terrors of the earth. You think I'll weep;
> No, I'll not weep:
> I have full cause of weeping, but this heart
> Shall break into a hundred thousand flaws
> Or ere I'll weep.

There, as the eighteenth century would subsequently say, speaks nature in her purest accent.

Yet, as everyone knows, this figure and his persecutors and allies move in a dense atmosphere of implication. Are there whispers of Apocalypse, as some think, on that heath where King, Fool, and Madman-Beggar congregate amid the sounds and images of doom? Is the hill that Gloucester is told he climbs a foretaste and brief map of Purgatory, as R. W. Chambers once suggested? [3] Do we see in the play's grand opening a rash choice merely or something more like an archetype of all choosing, a pattern of the mind's act of will as that act begins to grow and branch in the material world, locking subject to object on a wheel of fire? The play has qualities that seem to countenance our asking such questions, though nothing is clearer than the specificities by which at the same time it insists that Gloucester's cliff is neither in our own mythic imagination nor in his, but at Dover; that the mysterious heath is located on the fringes of an Elizabethan agricultural community; and that the chooser of the opening scene, whatever else he may be, is a foolish parent — "full of changes," as his elder daughters tell us, from whose "unruly waywardness that infirm and choleric years bring with them" starts of egotism and wilfulness are only to be expected. Here then are divided and distinguished worlds, bonded to each other in such an intimate way that it is idle to argue which takes precedence of the other. To neglect either — as onstage it has been the custom to neglect the parabolic dimension throughout most of the play's history — is to destroy the most remarkable compound of realism and artifice that Shakespearean dramaturgy ever achieved.

---

[3] *King Lear* (W. P. Ker Memorial Lecture), Glasgow University Publications, No. 54 (1940), p. 44.

II

Perhaps the clearest route to the aspect of *Lear* that belongs to parable is by way of its sources. In general, I think, discussions of Shakespeare's sources, in this play and others, have erred by defining the term too narrowly, paying almost exclusive attention to specific books — in the case of Lear, to Sidney's *Arcadia*, the old play, and two or three other works that may have contributed some details — while virtually ignoring larger, admittedly vaguer, but equally cogent influences, which frequently determine the way in which the specific source is used. It is difficult, for instance, to account for what Shakespeare made of the old play apart from the influence of some such governing archetypal theme as that embodied in folk and medieval renderings of the Abasement of the Proud King.[4] In one common form of this archetype, the king comes from swimming or his bath to find his clothes and retainers gone. His role has been usurped by an angel sent from heaven to teach him, in the words of the Magnificat, that God humbles the proud and exalts the humble. In his nakedness, he finds that the evidence of his kingliness, indeed his whole identity, is gone. Assertions that he is in fact the king and efforts to regain his throne lead those around

---

[4] For a full discussion of the main forms of this story see Lillian H. Hornstein, *"King Robert of Sicily*: Analogues and Origins," PMLA, LXXIX (1964), 13–21. The version summarized in this paragraph is Jean de Condé's *Le dis dou Magnificat*. In this the king travels first to one, then to the other, of his two brothers, seeking assistance, but he is recognized by neither. It should be noted that in none of the orthodox "sources" cited for *King Lear* is there any mention of madness. In the Abasement of the Proud King archetype, this feature is present, probably because, as Miss Hornstein shows, the archetype has roots in, or has at least been influenced by, Scriptural-Talmudic commentary, especially on the divine punishment of Solomon and Nebuchadnezzar.

him to mock him as a madman. Standing at last among the beggars outside his own palace, wind torn, tormented by hunger and thirst, he acknowledges his true position, repents his former arrogance, and is then enlightened by the angel and restored to power. As in *King Lear*, there is humbling of pride here, nakedness and beggary and madness, loss of "identity," suffering in the cold; there is also, in the story's point, the theme which Professor Muir rightly emphasizes in his edition of *King Lear* [5] as the governing conception of the scene where Goneril and Regan are tried by a "mad beggar, a dying Fool, and a serving man" — *He hath put down the mighty from their seat, and hath exalted the humble and meek*.

In the finest of all the retellings of this archetype,[6] the repudiated king is not driven out but made the court Fool and compelled to take his food with the palace dogs.[7] This is a detail that may (or may not) have something to do with Lear's hallucination in the farmhouse that "the little dogs and all, Tray, Blanche, and Sweetheart, see, they bark at me." In this version, the king's repentance comes when he has gone in the usurping angel's retinue to Rome, where to his dismay his former fellow-rulers, the Emperor and Pope, do not recognize him at all, and suppose him to be a mad fool. In a moment of insight the king sees a likeness between himself and the great Nebuchadnezzar who was also brought low and lived in a desert for many years on roots and grass.[8]

---

[5] Introduction p. xlviii.

[6] *King Robert of Sicily*: see *Middle English Metrical Romances*, ed. W. H. French and C. B. Hale, (New York, 1930), pp. 937 ff.

[7] Lines 163–168, 185–186, 198–206.

[8] One cannot but wonder whether the stories told in Scripture of the punishment of Nebuchadnezzar, who for his pride was driven mad and made to live on grass as a beast among the beasts, may not lie somewhere

He is moved to repentance and in his humble prayer acknowledges himself to be only "thy fool, Lord." In the past when asked who he is, he has "euere . . . seide he was lord." Now the angel asks the question again, and the reply comes: "A fool." On this, the angel reveals himself, and the king is restored.

This is one kind of generalized shaping influence that has not been sufficiently considered among the backgrounds of *King Lear*. Perhaps Shakespeare's own work is another. Though King Lear is not a political play, and obviously has heights and depths undreamed of in the histories, the analysis of authority still occupies a considerable place in it, and motifs come repeatedly to the surface that belong far more to Shakespeare's own historical enterprises than to the *True Chronicle History of King Leir*. The theme of shadow versus substance is broached first by Shakespeare in the opening lines of *2 Henry VI*, where Suffolk, Henry's proxy in espousing Princess Margaret of France on French soil, delivers up, in a speech bristling with prophetic ironies,

> my title in the Queen
> To your most gracious hands, that are the substance
> Of that great shadow I did represent.

Everybody will remember too the moment in *Richard II* when Richard shatters the looking glass in which he has been studying himself with the comment that his great sorrow has destroyed his face; and, when Bolingbroke remarks

---

in the background of Lear's madness, his fellowing with the wolf and owl, and his stress on man's life becoming "cheap as beast's" — as well, perhaps, as in the background of Edgar's pride-punishing, fiend-haunted dieting on the lowest forms of life. John Calvin's exegesis on the Nebuchadnezzar material in the Book of Daniel is suggestive in this connection, but far from conclusive.

that it is really only the shadow (or imagination) of sorrow that has destroyed the shadow of his face, is moved to a reply that looks ahead to both *Hamlet* and *King Lear*:

> 'Tis very true, my grief lies all within;
> And these external manners of laments
> Are merely shadows to the unseen grief
> That swells with silence in the tortur'd soul.
> There lies the substance.

It is from this kind of background surely that Lear's question — "Who is it who can tell me who I am" — and the Fool's reply — "Lear's shadow" — together with the play's profound insistence that "nothing" will indeed come of nothing derive their full meaning; even though Lear's comment to Perillus in the old play — "And think me but the shadow of myself" [9] — may be responsible for attaching the theme to the person of Lear.

The appeal to a basic humanity shared by king and peasant, and differentiated in the king's case only by appearances, by trappings, by "general ceremony," is another pervasive theme of the histories that has clearly helped to shape *King Lear*. In the histories, it comes out usually in the form of envy expressed by care-worn monarchs of the sleep of ship-boys, wretched slaves "crammed with distressful food," and "he whose homely brow with biggin bound Snores out the watch of night." Henry V gives it a larger scope the night before Agincourt as he goes incognito among his soldiers.

. . . I think the King is but a man, as I am. The violet smells to him as it does to me; the element shows to him as it doth to me; all his senses have but human conditions. His ceremonies laid by in his nakedness he appears but a man.

---

[9] Line 1111.

This discovery is made again on the heath by Lear, as everybody knows — but transformed now from a copybook "sentence" (approved food for regal reflection) to agonized self-recognition:

Ha! here's three on's are sophisticated; thou art the thing itself; unaccommodated man is no more but such a poor, bare, fork'd animal as thou art. Off, off, you lendings!

Perhaps even the history plays' conception of Riot or Appetite let loose upon the realm by some act of violation or transgression on the monarch's part is recapitulated in the way in which the anarchy of appetite represented by Goneril and Regan and Edmund is made to spread out like a cancer from Lear's present act of folly and Gloucester's adultery of long ago. Shakespeare has underscored this theme in the second cycle of his history plays by means of a subplot, and has recourse to the device again in *Lear*, the only play among his mature tragedies in which a subplot is used. If such comparisons tell us no more, finally, than how much broader the canvas is in *Lear* than in history or political play, they yet have their use in stressing the variety and complexity Shakespeare's invention is able to achieve from a comparatively limited repertory of well-tried ideas.

In some aspects of its structure, *Lear* was also influenced by procedures its author had found useful in the comedies. Curiously teasing, but too tenuous to pursue, is the apparent recollection of Launcelot Gobbo, with the "fiend" at his elbow and meeting his blind father, in Edgar; and, again, of the words of Bassanio, as he justifies choosing the leaden casket, in France's speech valuing Cordelia as "most rich, being poor." We come on firmer ground with the scuffle of Edgar and Oswald. Edgar at this point plays the role of a poor countryman, speaks in a rural dialect, wields a cudgel;

Oswald, who has been presented throughout the play as courtly, insinuating, servile, commands a sword. Yet Edgar kills him, and the event is usually taken to signify some sort of ascendancy of soundhearted "nature" over corrupt "nurture," such as is exemplified in the resistance of Cornwall's servant to the blinding of Gloucester and repeated at a higher level in Edgar's conquest of Edmund. Precisely such an "exemplary" combat Shakespeare had used before in *As You Like It*. There, Orlando, the unschooled country youth, meets Charles, the Court's professional wrestler, epitomizing in his easy victory the superiority of all those in the play who are blessed with Nature's goods over those who possess Fortune's, while at the same time foreshadowing the further successes of "Nature" and her followers in the forest of Arden.

Other comedies can of course be cited: there is hardly one that is not echoed at some point in *King Lear*, but rather because Shakespeare works and reworks tirelessly the same themes than because any specific episode has been molded by them. Thus *Measure for Measure* anticipates *Lear's* probing of the relations of justice to power; *Much Ado*, its emphasis on the self-deception of those who think themselves wise; *Twelfth Night*, its theme of wisdom in folly, its Fool with incommunicable secrets and a catch in his throat (in both senses of the word "catch"), and, in Malvolio, though here the sock is worn and not the buskin, the Hobbist thrust of Edmund. For what may be a more explicit and interesting relationship, we must turn to *All's Well*. In this play the old Lord Lafeu's encounter with Parolles, in which he ridicules the young swaggerer's finery, punctures his bravado, and shows only contempt for his manhood, looks as if it might have been the model for the encounter of Kent and Oswald in our play. Lafeu says:

I must tell thee, sirrah, I write man; to which title age cannot bring thee.

. . . By mine honour, if I were but two hours younger, I'd beat thee, Methinks thou art a general offence, and every man should beat thee. I think thou wast created for men to breathe themselves upon thee.

. . . You are more saucy with lords and honourable personages than the commission of your birth and virtue gives you heraldry. You are not worth another word, else I'd call you knave.

This is not quite Kent's accent, but it is very much his subject matter. And Parolles's reply that only respect for Lafeu's age — "the privilege of antiquity" — stays his hand from forceful retaliation anticipates the bluster of Oswald once he is under Cornwall's protection in *King Lear*: "This ancient ruffian, Sir, whose life I have spared at suit of his gray beard . . ."

The most interesting recollection of *All's Well* in *King Lear* for my purposes centers in Helena's comment on Parolles. Of him she speaks as kindly as she can because he is companion to her beloved Bertram. "I love him for his sake," she says:

> And yet I know him a notorious liar,
> Think him a great way fool, solely a coward;
> Yet these fix'd evils sit so fit in him,
> That they take place when virtue's steely bones
> Looks bleak i' th' cold wind.

The triumph of a corrupt pliancy over uningratiating rectitude that these lines sketch finds an objective visual correlative, I venture to think, when Oswald's "fix'd evils," after the quarrel with Kent, so take place with Goneril and Regan as to admit him to Gloucester's castle, while Kent — "virtue's steely bones," if ever man was — sits out the night in the stocks.

III

Kent in the stocks brings us back to that distinctive feature of *King Lear* with which we began: its combination of parable and parable situations with acute realism. The scenes of the play have something in common with those landscapes we occasionally meet with in its author's own country, all meadow or glebe to the normal view, but revealing under their green skin when seen from a neighboring hill, huge chalky symbols deriving from a habitation and culture centuries gone by. Some such dual awareness, one suspects, must have been present for Shakespeare's original audiences in many or most of its scenes, and Kent's being thrown into the stocks is an excellent case in point.

All could see and sympathize with Kent's visible *persona*, the loyal servant and ambassador of an imperious old man whose reaction to this insult to his majesty and parenthood would be apprehensively anticipated as matter for the coming scenes. But here onstage, at the same time, was an emblem, an archetype, a situation timeless and recurrent, catching in a mirror the world's way with virtue when separated from power. To some — those who knew their Bible best — it might bring reminiscences of the story of Paul and Silas, when by the magistrates of Philippi they were thrown into prison and the stocks, only to be miraculously released at midnight by an earthquake as they sat singing psalms; and doubtless these members of Shakespeare's audience would suppose they knew precisely what he meant (as no one else ever has) by Kent's reference to miracles when he says in soliloquy, "Nothing almost sees miracles But misery." To others, the scene might bring analogues more abstract: images of Virtue Locked Out, or of the Messenger of the King (or of the God) Turned Away, or of "Honesty . . . praised but left to freeze," as Juvenal has it in a famous line.[10] None would recall in 1606, nor would the playwright himself, that in a Morality play of about a century earlier Pity was thrown into the stocks and left to soliloquize on the evils of the time,[11] or that in another morality of about the same period Charity had been stocked by Riot and Pride with the aid of the hero Youth, who had rejected Charity's good counsel.[12] No one would recall these works in 1606, but the habit of thought they represented and the whole legacy of medieval culture of which they were part guaranteed the possibility that any episode, onstage or in life, might be taken as exemplary and emblematic, the more so if it suited with traditional patterns, or familiar incidents of the same sort.

King Lear, as everybody knows, is a treasury of such patterns and a tissue of such incidents. Lear himself, as Professor Harbage among others has pointed out — flanked in that opening scene by "vices or flatterers on the one hand, virtues or truth-speakers on the other" — [13] stirs memories of a far more ancient dramatic hero, variously called Mankind, Everyman, Genus Humanum, Rex Vivus, Rex Humanitas, Magnificence, etc. He is about to endure an *agon* that, while infinitely more poignant and complex than theirs, has its roots in the same medieval conception of psychomachia, interpreting man's life as "the arena of a Holy War between

---

[10] *Satire I,* line 74: probitas laudatur et alget.
[11] *Hickscorner (Tudor Facsimile Texts,* ed. J. S. Farmer [1908], leaves B2v–B3v).
[12] *The Interlude of Youth (ibid.,* leaf B4v).
[13] In his Introduction to the Pelican *King Lear* (1958), p. 22.

the contending forces of his own nature."[14] Somewhere in the deep background of the causes that call him to this trial may still lurk the notion of the Summons of Death, which sometimes precipitates the psychomachia in the early Morality plays — now lingering on only in the hint Lear gives that he has divided his kingdom, in order that he may "unburthen'd crawl toward death." The persons surrounding him are in some sense (again as in the Morality plays) extensions of himself, who will struggle to assist or defeat him, and most of them show a monolithic simplicity and singleness of being which makes them representative, as Bradley saw, of the Morality tendency "to decompose human nature into its constituent factors."[15]

Though the complexity of the play as a whole sets it worlds apart from this tradition, one cannot but be struck by the number of details in *King Lear* that seem to derive from it.[16] The opening scene, as noted, partly parallels an episode in most of the Moralities wherein one or more vices cloaked as virtues drive a wedge between the gullible hero and the virtues that support him. Lear's blind self-confidence on this occasion, though a trait of character, is also, one feels, the exemplary self-confidence of the Morality hero — proud man, "drest in a little brief authority," performing his tricks before a heaven in which it is not clear there are any angels left to weep. The road Lear soon must travel, like the road which

---

[14] Bernard Spivack, *Shakespeare and the Allegory of Evil: The History of a Metaphor in Relation to His Villains* (1958), p. 73.

[15] *Lectures on Shakespearean Tragedy* (1904), p. 264.

[16] As critics and editors have pointed out, the play contains a number of what seem to be glancing allusions to the morality tradition. See Spivack, *op. cit.*, p. 67, on Edmund's "and yet he comes, like the catastrophe in the old comedy" (I,ii,141-142); and the notes on II,ii,36 and III,vi,26-29 in Muir's Arden edition of the play.

Eugenio is advised to travel in the interlude *John the Evangelist* and which others will travel as far forward in time as Bunyan's pilgrim, includes psychological landmarks like the "mede of mekenesse," the "path of pacyence," the "lande of largenes"; [17] and though the places in Lear's pilgrimage are no longer, like these, known stages in a certified spiritual progress, and the heavenly destination is no longer clear, the sense of journey to some form of consummation remains.

One gathers there may be similarly persistent formulas in the background elsewhere. Lear's changed garments in the reconciliation scene bring to mind the new clothing brought to Skelton's Magnificence, after his repentance, by Redress.[18] His somewhat riddling words to Cordelia as they are about to be led to prison —

> He that parts us shall bring a brand from heaven
> And fire us hence like foxes —

may have reference to a kind of exit preserved for us in two surviving early plays, where the Vice is driven offstage by fire from heaven.[19] And at the moment of Lear's death, what seems to be a version of the old theme of Death's Summons reappears — not in Lear's own ending, but in Kent's reply to Albany:

> I have a journey, sir, shortly to go;
> My master calls me, I must not say no.

Gloucester's story, yet more continuously and clearly than Lear's, incorporates hints and fragments from the Morality

[17] Lines 95–97.

[18] *Magnyfycence*, lines 2402–2406.

[19] In Bale's *Three Laws* (*Tudor Facsimile Texts*, ed. J. S. Farmer [1908], leaf F5r) and in *King Darius* (*ibid.*, [1907] leaves F3r–F4v).

tradition. Like Mankind in the Morality of that name,[20] Gloucester is divided from one who truly cares for him by one who seeks only his destruction; like Everyman,[21] he is eventually forsaken by all save one guide, who comforts and accompanies him to the end; like Magnificence [22] in Skelton's interlude, he is tempted to suicide but survives through the dispelling of despair by hope. Again, as with Lear, the difference in Shakespeare's treatment must count most, yet the old conventions and techniques sometimes give us valuable perspective on this. Edmund, for instance, is seen more intelligently if he is seen in part as a figure whose name *could* be Appetite — sprung from his father's appetite and seeking to devour all that lies in his way: brother, father, mistress, the kingdom itself, precisely in the manner laid down by Ulysses in *Troilus and Cressida*:

> And appetite, an universal wolf,
> So doubly seconded with will and power,
> Must make perforce a universal prey,
> And last eat up himself.

Edmund's resentments at primogeniture (which he calls "the curiosity of nations"), at "dull, stale, tired" beds "creating a whole tribe of fops," and at the brand of bastardy applied by society to his kind strike us in the theatre as lively humanizing touches, and in fact they are; but the solid shape under the idiosyncratic accent remains that of the Vice figure of the Morality plays, who confides his scorn of virtue to the spectators in a similarly insinuating tone and always

---

[20] Lines 518 ff.
[21] Lines 486 ff.
[22] Lines 2284–2344.

identifies himself for them by attacking the moral bases of the life they lead.[23]

In Edmund's brother Edgar we see a character whose possible Morality backgrounds are still more various. His unblinking attitude toward his father's transgressions and his strict code of retribution, both expressed as his wicked brother lies dying under his judicial hand —

> The Gods are just, and of our pleasant vices
> Make instruments to plague us;
> The dark and vicious place where thee he got
> Cost him his eyes —

are less (one must think) characteristics of the solicitous and patient guide of Gloucester and the pitying observer of Lear than necessities of his role as presenter of legitimacy and polar opposite to his brother's Appetite.

On the other hand, in his scenes on the heath as Mad Tom, many of his words and actions relate him to the hero figure of the Moralities after this figure has fallen on evil days and ways. Perhaps this is designed to keep before us the inner metaphysical and moral cost of Appetite while the intervening scenes are exhibiting its gross outer efficiencies in the successful plot of Edmund against his father. At any rate, Edgar is attended by "fiends," who have misled him through a partly moralized landscape of "fire and flame," "bog and quagmire," [24] and has been tempted to suicide with knife and

---

[23] See Spivack, *op. cit.*, pp. 118 ff. and chap. vi, especially pp. 163 ff.; and J. F. Danby's comment on Edmund's first soliloquy in *Shakespeare's Doctrine of Nature* (1949), p. 32: "No medieval devil ever bounced on to the stage with a more scandalous self-announcement."

[24] Cf. the "marshe" which Eugenio in *John the Evangelist* must go through, Bunyan's Slough of Despond, the stagnant sea of the Ancient Mariner, etc.

halter, as happens often to the Morality hero.[25] Recollections of the Seven Deadly Sins, which he has practiced (III,iv,85–95), and of the Ten Commandments, which he now bids his hearers keep (III,iv,80–83,95–99), run through his wild chatter, in which we recognize at some moments the Morality theme of Pride and Corrupt Sensuality turned out of doors to grovel among the lowest living things for food (as in the story of Nebuchadnezzar alluded to earlier in conjunction with the Abasement of the King) and at other moments the outcast naked wretch who by virtue of total alienation has become indeed the thing itself — the "fork'd animal," the "worm."

Edgar's career in the play as a whole, especially after he has laid aside his madness, gives him a further kinship to one type of Morality hero — the naïf and dupe who out of deception and harsh experience gains wisdom. Toward the play's close this pattern becomes insistent. A formula summarizing Edgar's present stage of learning is presented three times, only to be followed at once by an experience that explodes it. He observes that to be mad Tom is to be at Fortune's nadir with no change possible except for the better, then meets his blinded father and knows "I am worse than e'er I was." He heals his father's despair at Dover Cliff, but finds him after the battle "in ill thoughts again" and ready to "rot" where he is. He pronounces judgment on his brother and on his father's act in begetting him, in full confidence, as we have heard him say, that "The gods are just," only to learn in a few moments that Cordelia has been hanged at the order of that brother and under the countenance of those

---

[25] These are standard temptations of the devil in all Morality-related literature, e.g. *Magnyfycence* (lines 2312–2315), *The Faerie Queene* (I,ix, 29), *Doctor Faustus* (V,i,60).

gods. His last speech in the play, if we follow the Folio text in giving the closing lines to Edgar rather than to Albany, is just possibly eloquent of what we are to think has taken place in him. The words ring no longer with high conviction; their form has little of the sententiousness that has characterized him earlier; and if in a sense they still sum up the play, it is because they carry a minimum of commitment:

> The weight of this sad time we must obey;
> Speak what we feel, not what we ought to say.
> The oldest hath borne most: we that are young
> Shall never see so much, nor live so long.

IV

There is one other defining "source" behind *King Lear*, I think. This is the shape of pastoral romance. What must have struck at least a few of Shakespeare's contemporaries as they watched the heath scenes was that here a scheme of things long associated with romance — in *King Lear*, as in romance, accompanied by disguises which actually deceive those who might be supposed most capable of seeing through them — is turned topsy-turvy and charged with unprecedented power. The action of most Renaissance pastoral romances is nearly as predictable as the action of an American western, which as everyone today knows, often fulfils a somewhat analogous function for its popular audiences. In the Renaissance versions, the protagonist moves out in a sweeping arc from the world of everyday, where he has confronted problems or experiences that threated to disintegrate him, to some sort of Arcadian countryside or forest, which is more fully in sympathy with human feelings and states. There he undergoes a learning process that consists in considerable part of discovering his own problem reflected in those he meets. Having viewed his problem in another, having sometimes undergone in the process something like a ritual death and rebirth, he is able to return to the everyday world, restored to serenity and often to temporal felicity. The broad characteristics of the pattern may be studied in Sidney's *Arcadia*, Montemayor's *Diana*, Sannazaro's *Arcadia*, and in such of Shakespeare's own works as *A Midsummer Night's Dream*, *As You Like It*, *The Winter's Tale*, *The Tempest*, and perhaps others. The pastoral land ordinarily proves to be, as Bruce Wardropper has said in his study of *Diana*, "a stage on the road from subnatural urbanity to supernatural spirituality." [26]

That the ground plan of *King Lear* has been affected by a version of this pattern may be seen from a closer glance at *As You Like It*. In both plays, we have an extruded ruler, and an ugly thunderhead of passion which closes the doors of "nurture" to the more sympathetic members of the *dramatis personae* and impels them to seek "nature." There is a wind which is urged to "Blow, blow" because it is not so biting as ingratitude, and a Fool, who knows he has been in a better place, but is loyal. There are rustic primitives, who in *As You Like It* are the comical William and Audrey, in *King Lear* Tom of Bedlam and the country people who figure in his mad talk. There are good and evil brothers, the good brother in both plays leading an old man — in *King Lear* his father, in *As You Like It* an old servant who has been a father to him; and there is a daughter of the extruded ruler, herself an exile, who is reunited to her father before the play ends.

Obviously, it is again the differences that count. Yet even the differences have a surrealistic resemblance. *As You Like*

---

[26] "The Diana of Montemayor: Revaluation and Interpretation," *Studies in Philology*, XLVIII (1951), 130.

It moves from extrusion to a magical forest, where everyone meets, as in a glass, reflections of what he is. To the good Duke, the forest discovers

> tongues in trees, books in the running brooks,
> Sermons in stones, and good in everything.

To Orlando, it discovers first a community of "kindness" — that is to say, natural feeling — when he meets the Duke and his men preparing food and is invited to partake. Such "kindness" is precisely what he has vainly sought at home, and what he himself exemplifies as he carries Adam on his back and forages sword in hand to feed him. Soon after this, the forest discovers love to Orlando. To Jaques, by contrast, the forest brings the stricken deer, abandoned and self-pitying like himself, whose "sobbing" he accompanies with his own "weeping." To Rosalind, it brings tongues in trees, but not in the same way as to her father: to her the trees speak of love and in rhyme; their "fruit" is Orlando, found by Celia under an oak "like a dropped acorn." Touchstone, as we might expect, unearths in the forest an Audrey; Silvius woos a Phoebe; Celia, who had given up everything to accompany Rosalind, meets with an Oliver, who has also learned by this time to give up. To each visitor, the forest brings according to his capacity; and following an exhibition of Rosalind's "magic," which some might wish to argue parodies the notion of a ritual death and rebirth (when she withdraws as Ganymede to reappear as Rosalind), all except Jaques and the newly arrived Duke Frederick leave Arcadia for the world.

King Lear alludes to such patterns, it seems to me, but turns them upside down. It moves from extrusion not to pastoral, but to what I take to be the greatest anti-pastoral ever penned. Lear's heath is the spiritual antipodes of the

lush romance Arcadias. Nature proves to be indifferent or
hostile, not friendly — yet curiously expressive, as in romance,
of the protagonist's mental and emotional states. The figures
are not Arcadian, but the wretched fiend-haunted villagers of
Edgar's hallucinations. The reflections of his condition that
Lear meets are barrenness, tempest, and alienation, the de-
fenseless suffering of his Fool, the madness of a derelict beggar who is "the thing itself." And though a "death" of sorts
occurs at the close of this anti-pastoral, followed much later
by hints of restoration and new beginnings when Lear is
brought onstage dressed in fresh garments and to the sound
of music, all that is thus won is no sooner won than snatched
away.

V

In the light of these back-
grounds in romance, Morality play, and possibly archetypal
folk motifs, certain identifying features of *King Lear* may,
I think, be more clearly apprehended. These features are not
peculiar to the play; they are characteristic of Shakespeare's
dramaturgy throughout his career; but the lengths to which
he here carries them, and their collective effect in combination, do give *Lear* a somewhat special status among the major
tragedies, as we may remember Margaret Webster pointing
out. One of these features, a clear inheritance from the backgrounds we have been discussing, is the presentation of characters, all of whom have at some time, and some of whom
have most of the time, a mode of being determined by what
they are and represent in the total scheme of the play rather
than by any form of psychic "life" fluctuating among "mo-
tives." The life of the Morality character, as Bernard Spivack
has ably pointed out, lies in "allegorical" motivation. The
character has *esse*, not *Existenz*: "What it does is what it has

to do by virtue of what it explicitly and indivisibly is." [27]
Morality characters, Spivack notes, continually act out their
esse, even when it is absurd for them to do so, as when Envy
in Medwall's *Nature* puts down his fellow vice Pride with a
lying trick for no other reason than that, in his own words,
"yt ys my guyse."

The complication in Shakespeare's management of character, whether in *Lear* or elsewhere, is simply that at any
given instant characters may shift along a spectrum between
compelling realism and an almost pure representativeness
that resembles (and evidently derives from) this *esse* of the
Morality play, though it is not necessarily allegorical. The
growth of Lear's passion in I,iv, culminating in his terrifying curse on Goneril, is conducted with a verisimilitude
whose effect in the theatre, it will be remembered, not even
Tate could spoil. Edgar stripping down to become Poor Tom,
on the other hand, obviously stands very near the pole of
representativeness. He acts out for us the forced alienation of
the good man (or at least the man more sinned against than
sinning) from security and civility in a corrupted world, a
theme which is to be repeated almost immediately, in a far
more realistic style, in the stocking of Kent, the repudiation
of Lear, and the expulsion of Gloucester. Through Edgar
we are given the "meaning" before we are given the event.
In the successive shifts of Lear's passion during the difficult
first scene of the play Shakespeare comes close to balancing
the two modes. There are hints of childishness, imperious-
ness, decaying powers, and incipient fury that the actor may
seize on and magnify to give a plausible body to Lear's test
of love and consequent folly, but there is also an *esse* in his
role which, like that of the Morality hero, *must* present itself

---

[27] *Op. cit.,* p. 127.

surrounded by forces of evil and good to which it is blinded by vanity and passion, *must* make a wrong choice and live to rue it, because that is the lot of man, and man's lot is the ultimate subject of the play.

Shakespearean character often has a corollary peculiarity, which in *King Lear* is allowed a good deal of scope. Its speech, despite the fact that it is often highly individualized, is always yet more fully in the service of the vision of the play as a whole than true to a consistent interior reality. Nicholas Brooke has pointed up this general Shakespearean practice shrewdly, instancing the speech of Ulysses on degree from *Troilus and Cressida*. "We *can* say about this," he observes, "that 'thinking, for such characters, is passionate experience,' and so seem to assimilate the thought to the character — but I question whether we shall believe ourselves":

The relevance to character is not "essential," it is very superficial; if we try to make it otherwise, we get some odd results. What is the character of the man that speaks this? A philosopher? What he offers is a commonplace resumé of what should have been "O" level material. He is an acute debater? [Rather, he is] a pompous and self-assertive bore, who should have been told to stick to the point, which was how to get Achilles to obey orders. A poet? No doubt, but out of season in a staff meeting on the battlefield. So what is the actor to do? Should he deliver the speech as a comic revelation of a pompous, poeticising, hectoring, tedious, overbearing fuddy-duddy? I have seen it done in just this way, disastrously.

But if one thinks of a different kind of character here, of the character of the speech, not the speaker, the result is surely very different: it is splendid and memorable. What should the actor do then? Speak it splendidly and memorably.[28]

---

[28] "The Characters of Drama," *Critical Quarterly*, VI (1964), 74. It is not of course Mr. Brooke's point, or mine, that speeches in Shakespeare's

This is precisely the relation that obtains between the character of Lear and his speech to a blind Gloucester in Dover fields about abuses of authority and excesses of sexuality. If we read it back into his *persona*, we wind up in Mr. Empson's position, appalled by an old man's "ridiculous and sordid" obsession.[29] This is particularly true onstage, where if we overstress by gestures and facial movements the psychic "authenticity" of Lear's lament, we lose altogether its emblematic and Morality-based dimension as a meditation or oration in the tradition of *De Contemptu Mundi,* with whose favorite illustration of man's miseries it closes: "We came crying hither. . . . When we are born, we cry that we are come To this great stage of fools."

A similar point must be made respecting the relation of character to action in Shakespeare, and particularly in our play. A Shakespearean *persona*'s action often has a species of transcendence that carries it beyond the plane on which such actions are acted or suffered in any imaginable real world of causes and effects. With the main "incentive" act of the drama, this is invariably the case: a brother's murder, a wife's or a mother's purity, a king's divinity, a child's ingratitude, will be invested by the play with all that a modern anthropologist would call *mana.* We do not know what Shakespeare thought of (say) adultery, as an ordinary Elizabethan human being whose experience of this particular sin (if we believe the evidence of the sonnets) may have been at first hand; but we know that his poet's imagination is capable of seeing in it, or in any other malefaction that threatens

---

plays are disembodied utterances; they are always spoken by a personality of some sort. I simply want to emphasize that the psychic distance between speaker and speech varies greatly, and nowhere more often than in *King Lear.*

[29] Above, p. 29.

the foundations of material and spiritual order, an assault upon the sum of things. "Heaven stops the nose at it, and the
moon winks," says Othello of what he believes to be his
wife's infidelity.

> Heaven's face doth glow,
> Yea, this solidity and compound mass
> With tristful visage, as against the doom,
> Is thought-sick at the act —

says Hamlet of his mother's. It is in this context that we must
consider the adultery of Gloucester. In one light it is merely
occasion for a seedy joke, an old man's cackle of sexual pride;
but in another it, too, is "the thing itself." To exclaim with
Mr. Empson (and a number of other critics who should
know better) that "even the resentful Edgar, and the sex-
resenting Shakespeare cannot have believed all through the
play that Gloucester deserved to have his eyes put out," [30] is
to miss the point. The punishment is exemplary like the act.
The blindness is not what will follow from adultery, but
what is implied in it. Darkness speaks to darkness.

Finally, we meet in *King Lear*, to a degree nowhere else
paralleled in Shakespeare's tragedies, a form of organization
that is as much homiletic as it is dramatic, and sometimes
more the former than the latter. We may see one aspect of
the play's homiletic bias in circumstances already mentioned
— the characters who are pure states of being, unmixedly
good and bad; or the scenes and episodes that have the quality of visual *exempla*, essentialized moments in a human history we all share, like Kent sitting in the stocks, Lear raving
in the storm, Gloucester taking his desperate leap, a madman

---

[30] *The Structure of Complex Words*, p. 150.

preaching to a blind man, etc. We may see another aspect of the bias in the fact that the play reverberates with preaching. The Fool preaches, Kent preaches, Albany preaches, Edgar preaches, and the two elder daughters preach at their father, so that when Lear finally says to Gloucester in Dover fields: "I will preach to thee: mark," it not only comes as a poignant climax, but makes us wonder whether the incoherence of his immediately succeeding utterances is not a reflection and summing up of the previous babble of creeds.

The full extent of the play's homiletic structure is seen best, however, by considering the Gloucester subplot. Gloucester's part in *King Lear*, as L. C. Knights has rightly insisted, "is not to give additional human interest, but to enact and express a further aspect of the Lear experience" — [31] or, as I would prefer to express it, to extend and consummate the play's wide-ranging vision of the nature and destiny of man. On this account, though the subplot's line of action sometimes crosses and even merges with that of the main plot in an external way, the relation of the two plots remains homiletic rather than dramatic: Gloucester's story is never permitted to discharge its full energies into the consciousness of Lear. The expulsion of Edgar; the fact that it is Edgar whom Lear meets on the heath as the thing itself; Edmund's rise to power, his relation with Lear's daughters, and his eventual defeat; Gloucester's blinding, expulsion, attempted suicide, and happy ending — these are all events of tragic import as we see them in the theatre, which come to Lear's attention only dimly (when they come at all) and make no part of his tragic experience. Their presence in the play is entirely dictated by their meaning for *us*.

---

[31] "The Question of Character in Shakespeare," *More Talking of Shakespeare*, ed. John Garrett (1959), p. 66.

This doctrinal relationship of one thing to another embraces almost every aspect of the play. It solidifies ideas into incidents, as Gloucester's blindness in I,ii, and Lear's madness in I,i, become physically fulfilled; or as Gloucester's appetite realizes itself in Edmund, and Lear's beggary in Edgar, his imperious isolation of the opening in the loneliness of the heath. Conversely, it bathes the literal event in figuration, so that Gloucester's imagined climb at Dover, to say nothing of his leap, teases the imagination. It also recapitulates episodes and speeches, even properties and gestures, making them reflect backward and forward on each other like the images in that succession of Platonic mirrors which are supposed to guide us from appearances to truth. Two thrones, for example, reflect back on the great one of the first scene: the chair or bench or joint stool that Lear occupies in the farmhouse when he tries his elder daughters, and the chair he occupies when he is carried in to awake in Cordelia's presence. If he sits down during his meditation *de contemptu mundi*, as I for one think he should, there will be a third throne to remind us of the first — perhaps a stone, perhaps (as in the Byam Shaw production for Laughton) some such suggestive seating as a straw bale near a haycart in a reaper's autumn landscape, making visible and palpable the "ripeness" that is all.[32] With no less poignant irony, Lear's kneeling before the power of Nature while he curses his eldest daughter (if the scene is played as Garrick played it) is repeated before Regan with a sarcasm that cannot conceal how much ground he has now lost with no compensating gain in practical insight.

---

[32] Muriel St. Clare Byrne, "King Lear at Stratford-on-Avon, 1959," *Shakespeare Quarterly*, XI (1960), 199.

Dear daughter, I confess that I am old;
Age is unnecessary: on my knees I beg
That you vouchsafe me raiment, bed, and food.

But the gesture then recurs with a wholly new dimension in
the reconciliation scene as Lear seeks to kneel to Cordelia;
and finally, in the hunched figure of the play's last moments
— who knows "when one is dead and when one lives," yet
still nurses the. human hope — it becomes an unforgettable
image of as much of the truth of man's fate as we shall ever
know for sure: that we love but to lose, that we grow in
goodness and understanding but to die.

Then there are the smaller dazzles of significance that these
recapitulations offer us, sometimes almost as breathtaking.
Cordelia's invocation of "all you unpublished virtues of the
earth" to be "aidant and remediate" in her father's distressed
state is made to shine out like a talisman (alas, in the long
run an insufficient one) against the dark powers Lear had
invoked in denouncing her and the destructive mission he
had assigned to Nature's powers in his curse of Goneril. The
"ripeness" brought to her lip by "patience and sorrow" striv-
ing "who should express her goodliest," and by her mingled
"smiles and tears" when she learns simultaneously that her
father is safe and how much he has suffered, casts a bright
light forward on the moment when Gloucester's heart, strug-
gling like hers between "two extremes of passion, joy and
grief," will burst "smilingly," and thus warns us that the
ripeness the play defines is not to be confused with maturity
that is only temporal. Again: Gloucester is led to his down-
fall by one deception, to some sort of salvation by another;
Edmund turns Gloucester against his brother with a forged
letter and Cornwall against Gloucester with a purloined letter, and is undone by an intercepted letter; masking his true

nature to deceive and defeat an unsuspecting brother in I,ii, Edmund meets the same brother masked in armor in V,iii, and is himself deceived and defeated. Such recapitulations, recurrences, and reverberations abound in *Lear*, as they abound everywhere in Shakespeare's work. The difference in *Lear* is that the cumulative effect is overwhelming. In *Lear*, even more than in *Macbeth*, significance holds plot and character in an iron grasp.

VI

The moral in all this for actors and directors is, I should think, obvious. Yet it is rarely drawn because the tides of psychological realism in our theatre continue to run strong.

In no staged play, it goes without saying, can we entirely dispense with the kind of characterization described by Miss St. Clare Byrne in her glowing review of the Byam Shaw–Laughton *Lear*. The Edmund, for instance, who is a "fine, smiling, young villain, with the necessary good looks and the sexual charm," who "plays himself into his opportunity with a cynical debonair relish that is almost likeable and makes him seem less dangerous than he is." [33] We cannot dispense with this nor should we want to. But in *King Lear* it is not enough. We need to be made aware also of the Edmund who is a force of Appetite and who in some sense seems *more* dangerous than he is because in recognizing his identity we recognize him in ourselves. This second Edmund cannot be found in speculations like those of Peter Brook and Charles Marowitz to the effect that Gloucester prefers Edmund to Edgar and is prepared to believe him against his brother because "he is a lusty and ambitious youth possessing the same

---

[33] *Ibid.*, pp. 201–202.

traits of zeal and flattery that probably raised Gloucester to his high court position." [34] This is to internalize and swallow up in an individualized psychology what Shakespeare has left a fluid combination of acts and speeches, hinting now at interior "motive" and now at external "significance." The actor who understands Shakespeare's Edmund will seek to convey to us something of both his modes of being, and the assignment will not be easy.

"He that plays the king," to borrow Hamlet's phrase, will have an assignment yet more difficult. The tendency here will equally be to simplify the role. Garrick, and most of his followers down through Laughton, have let the "portent" go, the great king who is also Rex Humanitas. Those who now play the play as an Elizabethan *Balcony* or *Waiting for Godot* are inclined to let the tottering parent go. As Marowitz has put it in a thoughtful final estimate of the production he helped direct:

I now suspect that the removal of *sympathy* and *identification* is the price we must pay for epic objectivity; that in forfeiting our conventional empathy for the poor old geezer tossed out on a stormy night by two cruel daughters, we prepare ourselves for the profounder emotionalism which comes from understanding the merciless logic of the play's totality: the realization that the tragedy is not Lear's but ours. [35]

Unquestionably this realization is part of Shakespeare's aim, and the main reason for his play's homiletic structure; but there is no evidence in the text that we are therefore to give over the "poor old geezer" in attaining it. On the contrary, as Shaw and Laughton observed in their interviews with Miss St. Clare Byrne,

---

[34] Marowitz, "*Lear* Log," p. 22.
[35] *Ibid.*, p. 32.

unless you have understood the savage, primitive rancor and hate-in-love of the "father against child, child against father" theme and followed its mounting crescendo from the exposition which is the rejecting of Cordelia to the clash which culminates in the curse on Goneril; unless you hear in that terrible curse the horrifying harshness of emotion that comes into an old voice when the speaker is wholly given over to the bitter, vindictive anger of hurt old age, so hurt that it would destroy its own parenthood by invoking sterility upon its child; and unless in the storm climax you understand the final blasphemy of fatherhood, which in its vengeful resentment, magnifying "filial ingratitude" to cosmic proportions, will "punish home" by calling down universal destruction; unless you have then realized how this gigantic, cumulative confession, this purging by utterance has emptied the heart of its poison, so that human contrition can enter in and with it illumination, you have not begun to grasp the play [that] Shakespeare wrote and that his own audience experienced. If you leave the theatre with a vague, uplifted feeling that you have been listening to the spirit of man defying the malice of the universe you might as well have stayed home.[36]

The problem is that Shakespeare's Lear is both the spirit of man and a rancorous father, just as Edgar is simultaneously a loving son, a choral device, a complement to Edmund, a voice of dislocation and disintegration in the storm, a thrust of hope and patience in Act IV, and possibly a *naïf* in process of learning throughout the play. Nothing in *King Lear* is entirely simple, not even the unmitigated badness of Goneril and Regan, which differs not only as between the two daughters, but in each daughter from one occasion to the next.

Finally, let us take a matter on which all productions have been agreed since at least the later eighteenth century, the

---

[36] *Op. cit.*, p. 205.

play's cast of primitivism. In that first scene, as any director knows, we must establish something bare, stark, faintly pagan, that will give countenance to Lear's oaths by Olympian gods and chthonic powers, and that will answer to and help support the folk-tale cast of the action here and the rude violence of all that follows. Yet we also need, and precisely in that same opening scene, to establish a deep sense of Renaissance England, whose typical figures so many of these are: the mighty King, the household Fool, the Machiavel or "new man" Edmund, the supple Oswald, the Bedlam beggar. And with this, we must establish a keen sense of sumptuousness and opulence, just the reverse of what is bare, stark, and primitive. We must behold a spectacle onstage that will accord with the play's stress on hierarchy and rank and give meaning to the gorgeousness attributed to Regan's clothing in II,iv, as well as to the furr'd gowns that "hide all" in Lear's meditations in IV,vi, and to Edgar's reduction from a rich exterior — in which we must not fail to recognize the marks of civility, nurture, and status — to

> The basest and most poorest shape
> That ever penury, in contempt of man,
> Brought near to beast.

We must have, in short, a powerful visual image of all that has to be put off to reach either the "nakedness" that Lear aspires to on the heath, or the plain (may we also say seamless?) garment which clothes him in the final scenes. This will not be an easy sense to give while we are stressing primitivism, and it may be that in this particular respect the actor's and director's "problem" with *King Lear* comes very close to being his dilemma.

In conclusion, the play calls for a performing style that has absorbed both epic disengagement and psychic intimacy, renders the implausible event plausible, moves easily from personification to personality, effectively marries the tragic to the absurd, and, above all, represses the urge to regularize and unify by twentieth-century psychological principles a play whose actual mode of unity is partly medieval and homiletic. This is a large order, but I think the very largeness of the order is perhaps our best clue to a possible way to meet it. What kind of experience (the actor or director might ask himself) are theatre audiences acquainted with that includes something like the fluidities and contradictions found in *Lear?* In what kind of world do we go on mysterious journeys of which we do not altogether understand the reason, arrive in places whose topography seems to be psychological and spiritual, commit actions and make gestures which have a profound ritual meaning, face logical improbabilities and indeed impossibilities with total equanimity, all in the company of persons whose reality is absolute yet seems to consist in something beyond themselves which after the experience is ended we can no longer recapture? In what world do people and events possess circumstantial reality for each of us, yet at the same time, if our psychologists are right, function "really" as huge cloudy symbols of a history generic to all human beings, whether we regard this history, with Freud, as a graph of psychological structure, or with Jung, as a repository of racial memory.

The answer to these rhetorical questions is, of course, dream. Not idle dreaming, but dream that is a form of truth: vision. This is what the Morality play was, a vision acted upon a platform whereby the invisible became visible and man's terrestrial pilgrimage was glimpsed whole in its entire arc of pride and innocence, temptation and fall, regeneration and salvation or ruin and damnation. This is also, essentially, what *Lear* is, save that in the case of *Lear* we must add to the arc of pilgrimage Shakespeare's more tragic vision of the creature whose fate it is to learn to love only to lose (soon or late) the loved one, and to reach a ripeness through suffering and struggle, only to die. If the contemporary director must seek a subtext for *King Lear*, I suggest the best place for him to find it is in a genre and mode of sensibility which has left its obvious mark on the play, and which, besides, through its own long and honorable tradition, from the Middle Ages to the present (in poetry and fiction as well as in drama), may still provide the best single clue to its conventions for the audiences of our time.

In the middle of the journey of our life I came to myself in a dark wood where the straight way was lost. Ah! how hard a thing it is to tell what a wild, and rough, and stubborn wood this was.

Then dreamt I a wondrous dream, that I saw all the world, and beheld on the east side a tower, and on the west a deep dale where Death dwelt. There was also a fair field, full of all manner of folk.

As I walked through the wilderness of this world, I lighted on a certain place, where was a Denn; and I laid me down in that place to sleep. And as I slept I dreamed . . . and behold *I saw a Man cloath'd with Raggs standing in a certain place, with his face from his own House, a Book in his hand, and a great burden upon his Back.*

Ye who listen with credulity to the whispers of Fancy, and pursue with eagerness the phantoms of hope; who expect that age will perform the promises of youth, and that the deficiencies of the present day will be supplied by the morrow; attend to the history of Rasselas prince of Abissinia.

rivverrun, past Eve and Adam's, from swerve of shore to bend of bay, brings us by a commodius vicus of recirculation back to Howth Castle and Environs.[37]

When we are given a *Lear* in the theatre that honors both its intimate humanity and its position in the company of such works as these, the problem of the play will have been solved. But not before.

---

[37] The quotations are the opening lines of the *Divine Comedy*, the *Vision of Piers Plowman* (the prose glosses), *Pilgrim's Progress*, *Rasselas*, and *Finnegans Wake*.

CHAPTER THREE

Action and World

Glou.	When shall I come to th' top of that same hill?
Edg.	You do climb up it now; look how we labour.
Glou.	Methinks the ground is even.
Edg.	Horrible steep: Hark! do you hear the sea?
Glou.	No, truly.
Edg.	Why, then your other senses grow imperfect By your eyes' anguish.
Glou.	So may it be, indeed.

I have tried to suggest in the foregoing pages some of the ways in which, and reasons on account of which, *King Lear* has been and is a problem — not simply to performers but to all who contemplate it closely. I have also ventured the proposition that more of the play becomes intelligible and significant if a view of it is taken that relates its conventions to literary modes to which it is genuinely akin, such as Romance, Morality play, and Vision, rather than to psychological or realistic drama, with which it has very little in common. This has been largely a historical undertaking.

I should like now to turn to some other aspects of *King Lear*, especially those which, as it seems to me, give it particular immediacy and impact for twentieth-century sensibilities. The other tragedies, to adapt Arnold's famous phrase, in a far larger degree abide our question: *King Lear* is free. It confronts us not only like Peter Brook's mountain, whose summit has yet to be scaled in performance, but like Hopkins's mountains of the mind —

> cliffs of fall,
> Frightful, sheer, no-man-fathomed —

where each exploration is also an exploration of ourselves.

For the abysses of the play are in fact wrapped in the enigma of our own ignorance of the meaning of existence, its peaks echo with cries of triumph and despair so equivocal that we are never sure they are not ours.

Doubtless one cause of the play's strong appeal today is that its "tragic-heroic" content, like that of most contemporary plays, is ambiguous and impure. This is not simply to refer to its well-known vein of grotesqueries, or those events and speeches which have the character of poignant farce and even of inspired music-hall fooling, like the Fool's mouthings, Edgar's gyrations, Gloucester's leap. The play does blur the ordinary tragic-heroic norms. Consider the death of the protagonist, for instance. This is usually in Shakespeare climactic and distinctive, has sacrificial implications, dresses itself in ritual, springs from what we know to be a Renaissance mystique of stoical self-dominion. How differently death comes to Lear! Not in a moment of self-scrutiny that stirs us to awe or exaltation or regret at waste, but as a blessing at which we must rejoice with Kent, hardly more than a needful afterthought to the death that counts dramatically, Cordelia's. To die with no salute to death, with the whole consciousness launched toward another; to die following a life-experience in which what we have been shown to admire is far more the capacity to endure than to perform: this is unique in Shakespeare, and sits more easily with our present sensibility (which is pathologically mistrustful of heroism) than the heroic resonances of the usual Shakespearean close.

The miscellaneousness and very casualness of death in *King Lear* is perhaps also something to which the generations that have known Hiroshima are attuned. In the other tragedies, as a student of mine has noticed in an interesting unpublished paper, there is always a hovering suggestion that death is noble, that the great or good, having done the deed or followed the destiny that was in them to do or follow, go out in a blaze of light. So Romeo and Juliet seem to go. So Cleopatra goes, turning to air and fire to meet Mark Antony. Hamlet goes in a glimpse of some felicity, Othello in a recollection of a deed of derring-do and justice, even Macbeth in a kind of negative glory like the transcendent criminal he has become. But *King Lear* repudiates this.

The dramatic emphasis is on the generality of death; death is not noble or distinctive; nearly every character dies and for nearly every sort of reason. The reiterated fact of the multiple deaths is processional in quality. It is like an enormous summarial obituary. The Fool disappears of causes mysterious; Oswald, tailor-made servant, is killed by Edgar; Goneril and Regan are poisoned and dagger-slain; Gloucester dies offstage of weariness, conflicting emotion, and a broken heart; Kent is about to die of grief and service; Edmund is killed by his brother in a duel; Cordelia dies (by a kind of mistake — "Great thing of us forgot!") at a hangman's hands; and King Lear dies of grief and deluded joy and fierce exhaustion. . . . Death is neither punishment nor reward: it is simply in the nature of things.[1]

To this we may add, I think, a third factor that brings *King Lear* close to our business and bosoms today. As we saw in the preceding chapter, intimations of World's End run through it like a yeast. In the scenes on the heath, the elements are at war as if it were indeed Armageddon. When Lear awakes with Cordelia at his side, he imagines that already apocalypse is past, she is a soul in bliss, he bound upon a wheel of fire. Appearing in the last act with Cordelia dead in his arms, he wonders that those around him do not crack

---

[1] From a paper by Evelyn G. Hooven of the Yale Graduate School in English.

"heaven's vault" with their grief, and they wonder in turn if the *pietà* they behold is "the promis'd end" or "image of that horror." These are but some of the overt allusions. Under them everywhere run tides of doomsday passion that seem to use up and wear away people, codes, expectations, all stable points of reference, till only a profound sense remains that an epoch, in fact a whole dispensation, has forever closed.

> The oldest hath borne most: we that are young
> Shall never see so much, nor live so long.

To this kind of situation, we of the mid-twentieth century are likewise sensitively attuned. I shall quote from another student, partly because the comment is eloquent, but chiefly because I think it is significant that everywhere in the fifties and sixties the young are responding to *King Lear* as never before in my experience. "Every great critic," this student writes,

from Johnson on . . . at some time or other begins to think of the sea. The most moving example of this common image, perhaps, is Hazlitt's: he speaks of the passion of King Lear as resembling an ocean, "swelling, chafing, raging, without bound, without hope, without beacon, or anchor," and of how on that sea Lear "floats, a mighty wreck in the wide world of sorrows." . . . The sea plays no direct part in the action. But the smell of it and the sound of it are omnipresent. The sea licks up at Dover relentlessly, its "murmuring surge" is endless and inescapable and everywhere — an archetype not of an individual drowning, but of the flooding of the world. *King Lear* is alive again: it is our myth, our dream, as we stand naked and unaccommodated, listening to the water rise up against our foothold on the cliff of chalk.[2]

---

[2] From a paper by Leslie Epstein, formerly of the Yale School of Drama.

This statement is incomplete. It leaves out of account the strong undertow of victory in the play which carves on those same chalk walls Lear's "new acquist" of self-knowledge and devotion to Cordelia, the majesty of his integrity and endurance, the invincibleness of his hope. These give to an audiences's applause at the close of a great performance a quality of exaltation. The statement is incomplete; but what it includes and what it leaves out both make clear why *King Lear* above all others is the Shakespearean tragedy for our time.

II

I turn now to a closer scrutiny of the play. In the remarks that follow I shall address myself primarily to three topics, which I believe to be both interesting in themselves and well suited to bring before us other qualities of this tragedy which stir the twentieth-century imagination. The first topic is the externality of Shakespeare's treatment of action in *King Lear*; the second is the profoundly social orientation of the world in which he has placed this action; and the third is what I take to be the play's dominant tragic theme, summed up best in Lear's words to Gloucester in Dover fields: "We came crying hither."

As we watch it in the theatre, the action of *King Lear* comes to us first of all as an experience of violence and pain. No other Shakespearean tragedy, not even *Titus*, contains more levels of raw ferocity, physical as well as moral. In the action, the exquisite cruelties of Goneril and Regan to their father are capped by Gloucester's blinding onstage, and this in turn by the wanton indignity of Cordelia's murder. In the language, as Miss Caroline Spurgeon has pointed out, allusions to violence multiply and accumulate into a pervasive image as of "a human body in anguished movement — tugged, wrenched, beaten, pierced, stung, scourged, dislocated, flayed, gashed, scalded, tortured, and finally broken on the rack."[3]

Miss Spurgeon's comment tends to formulate the play in terms of passiveness and suffering. But the whole truth is not seen unless it is formulated also in terms of agency and aggression. If the *Lear* world is exceptionally anguished, it is chiefly because it is exceptionally contentious. Tempers in *King Lear* heat so fast that some critics are content to see in it simply a tragedy of wrath. Unquestionably, it does contain a remarkable number of remarkably passionate collisions. Lear facing Cordelia, and Kent facing Lear, in the opening scene; Lear confronting Goneril at her house with his terrifying curse; Kent tangling with Oswald outside Gloucester's castle; Cornwall run through by his own servant, who warns Regan that if she had a beard he'd "shake it on this quarrel"; Edgar and Edmund simulating a scuffle in the first act, and later, in the last act, hurling charge and countercharge in the scene of their duel; the old king himself defying the storm: these are only the more vivid instances of a pattern of pugnacity which pervades this tragedy from beginning to end, shrilling the voices that come to us from the stage and coloring their language even in the tenderest scenes. The pattern gives rise to at least one locution which in frequency of occurrence is peculiar to *King Lear* — to "outface the winds and persecutions of the sky," to "outscorn the to-and-fro contending wind and rain," to "outjest his heart-struck injuries," to "outfrown false Fortune's frown." And it appears as a motif even in that pitiful scene at Dover, where the old king, at first alone, throws down his glove before an imaginary opponent — "There's my gauntlet, I'll prove it on a giant" —

---

[3] *Shakespeare's Iterative Imagery* (1935), p. 342.

and, afterward, when the blind Gloucester enters, defies him, too: "No, do thy worst, blind Cupid, I'll not love." So powerful is this vein of belligerence in the linguistic texture of the play that pity itself is made, in Cordelia's words, something that her father's white hairs must "challenge." Even "had you not been their father," she says in an apostrophe to the sleeping king, referring to the suffering he has been caused by his other daughters, "these white flakes did challenge pity of them."

It goes without saying that in a world of such contentiousness most of the *dramatis personae* will be outrageously self-assured. The contrast with the situation in *Hamlet*, in this respect, is striking and instructive. There, as I have argued in another place, the prevailing mood tends to be interrogative.[4] Doubt is real in *Hamlet*, and omnipresent. Minds, even villainous minds, are inquiet and uncertain. Action does not come readily to anyone except Laertes and Fortinbras, who are themselves easily deflected by the stratagems of the king, and there is accordingly much emphasis on the fragility of the human will. All this is changed in *King Lear*. Its mood, I would suggest (if it may be caught in a single word at all), is imperative. The play asks questions, to be sure, as *Hamlet* does, and far more painful questions because they are so like a child's, so simple and unmediated by the compromises to which much experience usually impels us: "Is man no more than this?" "Is there any cause in nature that makes these hard hearts?" "Why should a dog, a horse, a rat have life And thou no breath at all?" Such questionings in *King Lear* stick deep, like Macbeth's fears in Banquo.

Yet it is not, I think, the play's questions that establish its

---

[4] "The World of Hamlet," *The Yale Review*, XLI (1952), 502-523.

distinctive coloring onstage. (Some of its questions we shall return to later.) It is rather its commands, its invocations and appeals that have the quality of commands, its flat-footed defiances and refusals: "Come not between the dragon and his wrath." "You nimble lightnings, dart your blinding flames into her scornful eyes!" "Blow, winds, and crack your cheeks! rage! blow!" "Thou shalt not die; die for adultery, no!" "A plague upon you, murderers, traitors, all! I might have sav'd her . . ." In the psychological climate that forms round a protagonist like this, there is little room for doubt, as we may see from both Lear's and Goneril's scorn of Albany. No villain's mind is inquiet. Action comes as naturally as breathing and twice as quick. And, what is particularly unlike the situation in the earlier tragedies, the hero's destiny is self-made. Lear does not inherit his predicament like Hamlet; he is not duped by an antagonist like Othello. He walks into disaster head on.

This difference is of the first importance. *King Lear*, to follow R. W. Chambers in applying Keats's memorable phrase, is a vale of soul-making,[5] where to all appearances the will is agonizingly free. As if to force the point on our attention, almost every character in the play, including such humble figures as Cornwall's servant and the old tenant who befriends Gloucester, is impelled soon or late to take some sort of stand — to show, in Oswald's words, "what party I do follow." One cannot but be struck by how much positioning and repositioning of this kind the play contains. Lear at first takes up his position with Goneril and Regan, France and Kent take theirs with Cordelia, Albany takes his with Goneril, and Gloucester (back at his own house), with Cornwall

---

[5] *King Lear* (W. P. Ker Memorial Lecture), p. 48.

and Regan. But then all reposition. Kent elects to come back as his master's humblest servant. The Fool elects to stay with the great wheel, even though it runs downhill. Lear elects to become a comrade of the wolf and owl rather than return to his elder daughters. Gloucester likewise has second thoughts and comes to Lear's rescue, gaining his sight though he loses his eyes. Albany, too, has second thoughts, and lives, he says, only to revenge those eyes. In the actions of the old king himself, the taking of yet a third position is possibly implied. For after the battle, when Cordelia asks, "Shall we not see these daughters and these sisters?" Lear replies (with the vehemence characteristic of him even in defeat), "No, no, no, no!" and goes on to build, in his famous following lines, that world entirely free of pugnacity and contentiousness in which he and Cordelia will dwell: "We two alone will sing like birds i' th' cage."

Movements of the will, then, have a featured place in *King Lear*. But what is more characteristic of the play than their number is the fact that no one of them is ever exhibited to us in its inward origins or evolution. Instead of scenes recording the genesis or gestation of an action — scenes of introspection or persuasion or temptation like those which occupy the heart of the drama in *Hamlet, Othello*, and *Macbeth* — *King Lear* offers us the moment at which will converts into its outward expressions of action and consequence; and this fact, I suspect, helps account for the special kind of painfulness that the play always communicates to its audiences. In *King Lear* we are not permitted to experience violence as an externalization of a psychological drama which has priority in both time and significance, and which therefore partly palliates the violence when it comes. This is how we do experience, I think, Hamlet's vindictiveness to his mother, Macbeth's massacres, Othello's murder: the act in the outer world is relieved of at least part of its savagery by our understanding of the inner act behind it. The violences in *King Lear* are thrust upon us quite otherwise — with the shock that comes from evil which has nowhere been inwardly accounted for, and which, from what looks like a studiedly uninward point of view on the playwright's part, must remain unaccountable, to characters and audience alike: "Is there any cause in nature that makes these hard hearts?"

III

The relatively slight attention given in *King Lear* to the psychological processes that ordinarily precede and determine human action suggests that here we are meant to look for meaning in a different quarter from that in which we find it in the earlier tragedies. In *Hamlet*, Shakespeare had explored action in its aspect of dilemma. Whether or not we accept the traditional notion that Hamlet is a man who cannot make up his mind, his problem is clearly conditioned by the unsatisfactory nature of the alternatives he faces. Any action involves him in a kind of guilt, the more so because he feels an already existing corruption in himself and in his surroundings which contaminates all action at the source. "Virtue cannot so inoculate our old stock but we shall relish of it." Hence the focus of the play is on those processes of consciousness that can explain and justify suspension of the will. In *Othello*, by contrast, Shakespeare seems to be exploring action in its aspect of error. Othello faces two ways of understanding love: Iago's and Desdemona's — which is almost to say, in the play's terms, two systems of valuing and two ways of being — but we are left in no doubt that one of the ways is wrong. Even if we take Iago and Desdemona, as some critics do, to be dramatic emblems of conflicting aspects in Othello's own nature, the play remains a tragedy of error, not a tragedy of dilemma. "The pity of it, Iago" is that Othello makes the wrong choice when the right one is open to him and keeps clamoring to be known for what it is even to the very moment of the murder. The playwright's focus in this play is therefore on the corruptions of mind by which a man may be led into error, and he surrounds Iago and Desdemona with such overtones of damnation and salvation as ultimately must attend any genuine option between evil and good.

King Lear, as I see it, confronts the perplexity and mystery of human action at a later point. Choice remains in the forefront of the argument, but its psychic antecedents have been so effectively shrunk down in this primitivized world that action seems to spring directly out of the bedrock of personality. We feel sure no imaginable psychological process could make Kent other than loyal, Goneril other than cruel, Edgar other than "a brother noble." Such characters, as we saw earlier, are qualities as well as persons: their acts have consequences but little history. The meaning of action here, therefore, appears to lie rather in effects than in antecedents, and particularly in its capacity, as with Lear's in the opening scene, to generate energies that will hurl themselves in unforeseen and unforeseeable reverberations of disorder from end to end of the world.

The elements of that opening scene are worth pausing over, because they seem to have been selected to bring before us precisely such an impression of unpredictable effects lying coiled and waiting in an apparently innocuous posture of affairs. The atmosphere of the first episode in the scene, as many a commentator has remarked, is casual, urbane, even relaxed. In the amenities exchanged by Kent and Gloucester, Shakespeare allows no hint to penetrate of Gloucester's later agitation about "these late eclipses," or about the folly of a king's abdicating his responsibilities and dividing up his power. We are momentarily lulled into a security that is not immediately broken even when the court assembles and Lear informs us that he will shake off all business and "unburthen'd crawl toward death." I suspect we are invited to sense, as Lear speaks, that this is a kingdom too deeply swaddled in forms of all kinds — too comfortable and secure in its "robes and furr'd gowns"; in its rituals of authority and deference (of which we have just heard and witnessed samples as Gloucester is dispatched offstage, the map demanded, and a "fast intent" and "constant will" thrust on our notice by the king's imperious personality); and in its childish charades, like the one about to be enacted when the daughters speak. Possibly we are invited to sense, too, that this is in some sort an emblematic kingdom — almost a paradigm of hierarchy and rule, as indeed the scene before us seems to be suggesting, with its wide display of ranks in both family and state. Yet perhaps too schematized, too regular — a place where complex realities have been too much reduced to formulas, as they are on a map: as they are on that visible map, for instance, on which Lear three times lays his finger in this scene ("as if he were marking the land itself," says Granville-Barker), while he describes with an obvious pride its tidy catalogue of "shadowy forests" and "champains," "plenteous rivers and wide-skirted meads." Can it be that here, as on that map, is a realm where everything is presumed to have been charted, where all boundaries are believed known, including those of nature and human nature; but where no account has been taken of the heath which lies in all countries and in all men and women just beyond the boundaries they think they know?

However this may be, into this emblematic, almost dream-like situation erupts the mysterious thrust of psychic energy that we call a choice, an act; and the waiting coil of consequences leaps into threatening life, bringing with it, as every act considered absolutely must, the inscrutable where we had supposed all was clear, the unexpected though we thought we had envisaged all contingencies and could never be surprised. Perhaps it is to help us see this that the consequences in the play are made so spectacular. The first consequence is Lear's totally unlooked-for redistribution of his kingdom into two parts instead of three, and his rejection of Cordelia. The second is his totally unlooked-for banishment of his most trusted friend and counselor. The third is the equally unlooked-for rescue of his now beggared child to be the Queen of France; and what the unlooked-for fourth and fifth will be, we already guess from the agreement between Goneril and Regan, as the scene ends, that something must be done, "and i' th' heat." Thereafter the play seems to illustrate, with an almost diagrammatic relentlessness and thoroughness, the unforeseen potentials that lie waiting to be hatched from a single choice and act: nakedness issues out of opulence, madness out of sanity and reason out of madness, blindness out of seeing and insight out of blindness, salvation out of ruin. The pattern of the unexpected is so completely worked out, in fact, that, as we noticed in the preceding chapter, it appears to embrace even such minor devices of the plot as the fact that Edmund, his fortune made by two letters, is undone by a third.

Meantime, as we look back over the first scene, we may wonder whether the gist of the whole matter has not been placed before us, in the play's own emblematic terms, by Gloucester, Kent, and Edmund in that brief conversation with which the tragedy begins. This conversation touches on two actions, we now observe, each loaded with menacing possibilities, but treated with a casualness at this point that resembles Lear's in opening his trial of love. The first action alluded to is the old king's action in dividing his kingdom, the dire effects of which we are almost instantly to see. The other action is Gloucester's action in begetting a bastard son, and the dire effects of this will also speedily be known. What is particularly striking, however, is that in the latter instance the principal effect is already on the stage before us, though its nature is undisclosed, in the person of the bastard son himself. Edmund, like other "consequences," looks tolerable enough till revealed in full: "I cannot wish the fault undone, the issue of it being so proper," says Kent, meaning by proper "handsome"; yet there is a further dimension of meaning in the word that we will only later understand, when Edgar relates the darkness of Edmund to the darkness wherein he was got and the darkness he has brought to his father's eyes. Like other consequences, too, Edmund looks to be predictable and manageable — in advance. "He hath been out nine years," says Gloucester, who has never had any trouble holding consequences at arm's length before, "and away he shall again." Had Shakespeare reflected on the problem consciously — and it would be rash, I think, to be entirely sure he did not — he could hardly have chosen a more vivid way of giving dramatic substance to the unpredictable relationships of act and consequence than by this confrontation of a father with his unknown natural son — or to the idea of consequences come home to roost, than by this quiet youthful figure, studying "deserving" as he prophetically calls it, while he waits upon his elders.

In *King Lear* then, I believe it is fair to say, the inscrutability of the energies that the human will has power to release is one of Shakespeare's paramount interests. By the inevitable laws of drama, this power receives a degree of emphasis in all his plays, especially the tragedies. The difference in *King Lear* is that it is assigned the whole canvas. The crucial option, which elsewhere comes toward the middle of the plot, is here presented at the very outset. Once taken, everything that happens after is made to seem, in some sense, to have been set in motion by it, not excluding Gloucester's recapitulation of it in the subplot. Significantly, too, the act that creates the crisis, the act on which Shakespeare focuses our dramatic attention, is not (like Lear's abdication) one which could have been expected to germinate into such a harvest of disaster. The old king's longing for public testimony of affection seems in itself a harmless folly: it is not an outrage, not a crime, only a foolish whim. No more could Cordelia's death have been expected to follow from her truthfulness or Gloucester's salvation to be encompassed by a son whom he disowns and seeks to kill.

All this, one is driven to conclude, is part of Shakespeare's point. In the action he creates for Lear, the act of choice is cut loose not simply from the ties that normally bind it to prior psychic causes, but from the ties that usually limit its workings to commensurate effects. In this respect the bent of the play is mythic: it abandons verisimilitude to find out truth, like the story of Oedipus; or like the *Rime of the Ancient Mariner*, with which, in fact, it has interesting affinities. Both works are intensely emblematic. Both treat of crime and punishment and reconciliation in poetic, not realistic, terms. In both the fall is sudden and unaccountable, the penalty enormous and patently exemplary. The willful act of the mariner in shooting down the albatross has a nightmarish inscrutability like Lear's angry rejection of the daughter he loves best; springs from a similar upsurge of egoistic willfulness; hurls itself against what was until that moment a natural "bond," and shatters the universe. Nor do the analogies end with this. When the mariner shoots the albatross, the dark forces inside him that prompted his deed project themselves and become the landscape, so to speak, in which he suffers his own nature: it is his own alienation, his own waste land of terror and sterility that he meets. Something similar takes place in Shakespeare's play. Lear, too, as we saw earlier, suffers his own nature, encounters his own heath, his own storm, his own nakedness and defenselessness, and by this experience, like the mariner, is made another man.

IV

To turn from a play's action to its world is not, when the dramatist is Shakespeare, to take up a new subject but to reconsider the old in a new light. The strains of violence and aggression stressed earlier in connection with the play's action could as well be treated as an aspect of its world. The bareness and spareness so often cited as features of its world penetrate equally the character and action. The austerity and rigor that these have in *King Lear* may best be appreciated by comparing Hal and Falstaff, in whom the dramatist's exuberant invention multiplies variety, to Lear and his Fool, where invention plays intensely but always along the same arc; or by recalling *Othello*, with all its supernumerary touches of actual domesticity in Desdemona, actual concerns of state in the Moor; or *Hamlet*, with its diversions and digressions among guardsmen, recorders, gossip of city theatres, its mass of historical and literary allusions, its diversities of witty, sophisticated, and self-conscious speech. Lear, too, contains diversities of speech — ritual and

---

⁶ "The Two Techniques in *King Lear*," *Review of English Studies*, XVIII (1942), 1–26, reprinted in enlarged form as chap. iii of his *Shakespeare and Spenser* (1950).

realistic styles described by W. B. C. Watkins,[6] iterations singled out by Bradley to characterize Cordelia [7] (which are, in fact, characteristic of several of the play's speakers), "oracular fragments of rhapsody" in the mad scenes (the phrase is Granville-Barker's),[8] imperatives, preachments, questionings, and, last but not least, the Fool's wry idiom, vehicle of the hard-won wisdom of the poor, made up largely of proverb, riddle, maxim, fable, and ballad. *Lear* has such diversities, but as Winifred Nowottny argues convincingly in a recent essay, all are marked, even the most passionate and poignant, by a surface "absence of contrivance," [9] which allows flashes of profound feeling to flare up unexpectedly in the most unpretentious forms of speech, yet seems to tell us at the same time (this is of course the measure of its artfulness in fact) that "feeling and suffering . . . are beyond words." "The play is deeply concerned," she writes, "with the inadequacy of language to do justice to feeling or to afford any handhold against abysses of iniquity and suffering." [10] Here, too, it strikes me, the play is of a piece. As it uses for the most part the barest bones of language to point at experiences that lie beyond the scope of language, so it uses stripped-down constituents of personality (character that is entirely *esse*, that does not alter but develops to be always more completely the thing it was — as in Kent, for whom banishment simply means that he will "shape his old course in a country new," and who at the end of the play will be about answering his master's call once again) to point to complexities of being

---

[7] *Lectures on Shakespearean Tragedy* (1904), p. 319; he is corrected on this point by Granville-Barker (*Prefaces to Shakespeare*, I, 281).

[8] *Ibid.*

[9] "Some Aspects of the Style of *King Lear*," *Shakespeare Survey*, XIII (1960), 51.

[10] *Ibid.*, p. 52.

and of human reality that lie beyond the scope of the ordinary conventions of dramatic character.

But these are matters that come through to us more clearly in the study than onstage. There can be no question that the most powerful single dimension of the play's world for its spectators is its continual reference to and evocation, through eye and ear alike, of the nature and significance of human society. A "sense of sympathy and human relatedness," as Miss Welsford has said, is what the good in this play have or win through to.[11] In the world of *King Lear*, this is the ultimate gift, spring of man's joy and therefore of his pain. When Lear dies, as I mentioned in the beginning, with his whole being launched toward another, with even his last gasp an expression of hope that she lives, the image before us is deeply tragic; yet it is also, in the play's terms, a kind of victory. This is a matter we must come back to. What needs to be considered first is the circumstantial "sociality" of the Lear world which defines and gives body to this closing vision of human achievement and its cost.

In writing *King Lear*, Shakespeare's imagination appears to have been so fully oriented toward presenting human reality as a web of ties commutual that not only characterization and action, but language, theme, and even the very *mise en scène* are influenced. The play's imagined settings — divisible into several distinct landscapes as "shadowy forests" and "champains" fade off first into "low farms and poor pelting villages," then into the bare and treeless heath, then into glimpses of high-grown grain at Dover on the brink of the giddy cliff that only exists in Edgar's speech and his father's imagination — are always emphatically social. Even on that

---

[11] *The Fool: His Social and Literary History* (1935), p. 258.

literally and emblematically lonesome heath we are never allowed to forget the nearby presence of what Mr. Eliot calls
in his *Dry Salvages* "the life of significant soil." Somewhere
just beyond the storm's rim and suitably framing the rain-
swept beggared king, Shakespeare evokes through Tom of
Bedlam's speeches a timeless community of farms and villages where the nights are measured between "curfew" and
"the first cock," the beggars are "whipp'd from tithing to
tithing," the green mantle of the standing pool is broken by
the castaway carcasses of the "old rat and the ditch dog," and
the white wheat is mildewed by "the foul Flibbertigibbet,"
who also gives poor rustics "the web and the pin, squinies the
eye and makes the hairlip." [12] Likewise at Dover, around
the two old men, one mad, one blind, Shakespeare raises another kind of society, equally well adapted to the movement
of the plot, courtly, sophisticated, decadent. A society of adul-
terers and "simp'ring dames." A society where "a dog's
obey'd in office," the beadle lusts for the whore he whips,
"the usurer hangs the cozener," and "robes and furr'd gowns
hides all."

It is by these surrealist backgrounds and conflations, as
we all know, that Shakespeare dilates his family story into
a parable of society of all times and places. The characters,
too, bear some signs of having been shaped with such a parable in view. As a group, they are significantly representative,
bringing before us both extremes of a social and political
spectrum (monarch and beggar), a psychic spectrum (wise
man and fool), a moral spectrum (beastly behavior and an-
gelic), an emotional spectrum (joy and despair), and,
throughout, a "contrast of dimension," as Miss Nowottny

---

[12] Evoked also, of course, is the society of Edgar's imagined corrupt past,
a society of "brothels," "plackets," "lenders' books," etc.

has called it,[13] that draws within one compass both the ut-
termost human anguish which speaks in "She's dead as
earth" and the strange limiting "art of our necessities" which
speaks in "Undo this button." As individuals, on the other
hand, these same characters, especially the younger ones,
show a significant and perhaps studied diversification. According to one producer of the play, we meet with "heartless
intellect" in Edmund, "impure feelings" in Goneril, "unen-
lightened will" in Cornwall, "powerless morality" in Albany,
"unimaginative mediocrity" in Regan.[14] I should not care
myself to adopt these particular descriptions, but they serve
to call attention to what everyone has recognized to be a
somewhat schematic variety in the play's *dramatis personae*,
as if the playwright were concerned to exhibit the widest possible range of human potentiality. This general "anatomy"
of mankind, if it is such, is further enhanced by the well-
known antiphonal characterizations of Lear and Gloucester
and even by the double quality of the old king himself as
Titan and (in Cordelia's phrase) "poor *perdu.*" Thus, from
the play's opening moments, when we are shown all the
powers of the realm collected and glimpse both aspects of
the king, we are never allowed to lose sight of the fact that
the people in front of us make up a composite image of the
state of man, in every sense of the word "state."

V

Shakespeare's concern with
"relation" as the ultimate reality for human beings also ex-
presses itself strongly in the plot of *King Lear* and in the

---

[13] *Op. cit.*, p. 56.

[14] Michael Chekhov, *To the Actor on the Technique of Acting* (1953), p.
134.

language of social use and habit to which the plot gives rise and which it repeatedly examines. To an extent unparalleled in the other tragedies, the plot of the play depends on and manipulates relations of service and of family — the two relations, as W. H. Auden has reminded us in an arresting essay, from which all human loyalties, and therefore all societies, derive.[15] Family ties, which come about by nature, cannot be dissolved by acts of will: in this lies the enormity of Lear's action in the opening scene and of his elder daughters' actions later. Service ties, however, being contractual, *can* be dissolved by acts of will, only the act must be ratified on both sides. Kent, refusing to dissolve his relation with his master, illustrates the crucial difference between the two types of affiliation. The essentials of the service bond can be restored even though Kent is unrecognized and in disguise. The essentials of the natural bond between Cordelia and Lear, or Edgar and Gloucester, can never be restored apart from mutual recognition and a change of heart.

Ties of service and ties of nature lie closely parallel in *King Lear* and sometimes merge. It has been argued that one way of interpreting the broad outlines of the story would be to say that the lesson King Lear must learn includes the lesson of true service, which is necessarily part of the lesson of true love.[16] Once Lear has banished true love and true service in the persons of Cordelia and Kent, it is only to be expected that he will have trouble with false service and false love in a variety of forms, including Oswald, his daughters, and his knights, and that he should need, once again, the intercession of true service in the form of the disguised Kent. Gloucester,

---

[15] "Balaam and His Ass," *The Dyer's Hand* (1962), pp. 107–108.
[16] Jonas Barish and Marshall Waingrow, " 'Service' in *King Lear*," *Shakespeare Quarterly*, IX (1958), 347–355.

too, we are told, has to learn to distinguish true service. Beginning by serving badly, he is badly served in turn by Edmund, and only after he becomes a true servant, going to Lear's rescue at the risk of his life, is he himself once more served truly, first by his old tenant, and subsequently by Edgar.

The term "service," with its cognates and synonyms, tolls in the language of *King Lear* like that bell which reminded John Donne we are all parts of a single continent, but it is only one of a host of socially oriented terms to do so. Almost as prominent, and equally pertinent to the playwright's concern with human relatedness, are the generic terms of social responsibility: "meet," "fit," "proper," "due," "duty," "bond," and the generic appellations of social status and social approbation and disapprobation: "knave," "fool," "villain," "rogue," "rascal," "slave," and many more. Often these last are simply vehicles of the willfulness that crackles in this frantic disintegrating realm where kings are beggars, but several of them carry in solution anxious questions about the ties that hold together the human polity, which from time to time the action of the play precipitates out. When Cornwall, challenged by his own servant after Gloucester's blinding, exclaims incredulously "My villain!" and Regan adds scornfully "A peasant stand up thus!" the ambiguities that may attach to servitude are brought into question with a precision that enables us to appreciate the immediately following references to Gloucester as "treacherous villain" and "eyeless villain," and to the now slain rebel servant as "this slave." In the Byam Shaw production, as Muriel St. Clare Byrne describes it, a highly imaginative *exeunt* was adopted for Regan and Cornwall at this moment, which must have brought home to any audience the implications of a world in which language could be so perversely and solipsistically misused.

"Mortally wounded, terror and pain in voice and gesture, Cornwall turned to his wife: 'Regan, I bleed apace. Give me your arm.' Ignoring him, almost disdainfully, she swept past to the downstage exit. He staggered back, groping for support; no one stirred to help him. Open-mouthed, staring-eyed, death griping his heart, he faced the dawning horror of retribution as the jungle law of each for himself caught up on him and he knew himself abandoned even by his wife." [17]

Two other "titles" that the play first manipulates and then explores in visually expressive episodes are "gentleman" and "fellow." Kent is introduced to us and to Edmund as "this noble gentleman" in the first lines of the play, a title which he later amplifies into "gentleman of blood and breeding." Oswald is also introduced to us first as a gentleman — "my gentleman" — by Goneril, and receives the title again at a significant moment when Edgar, speaking as a peasant, has to defend his father's life against him. In II,ii, these two very different definitions of gentility, Oswald and Kent, clash outside Gloucester's castle. The "gentleman of blood and breeding" puts Goneril's "gentleman" to rout by power of nature, but by power of authority — that great graven image of authority which, as Lear says later in a reference likely to recall this episode, makes "the creature run from the cur" — he is ejected (and punished) in favor of one whose true titles, Kent tells us, make him no gentleman, but "the composition of a knave, beggar, coward, pandar, and the son and heir of a mongrel bitch."

Or again, the play asks (and this is perhaps its most searching exploration visually as well as verbally), what is it that makes a man a "fellow"? Is it being born to menial status,

---

[17] *King Lear* at Stratford-on-Avon, 1959," *Shakespeare Quarterly*, XI (1960), 198.

as for the many servingmen to whom the word is applied? Is it total loss of status, as for Edgar, Kent, and Lear, to each of whom the word is also applied? Or is it simply being man — everyone's fellow by virtue of a shared humanity? During the heath scenes, when Lear, Kent, Edgar, and the Fool become fellows in misery as well as in lack of status, this question too is given a poignant visual statement. Gloucester, coming to relieve Lear, rejects one member of the motley fellowship, his own son Poor Tom: "In, fellow, there into the hovel." But Lear, who has just learned to pray for all such naked fellows, refuses to be separated from his new companion and finally is allowed to "take the fellow" into shelter with him. For, as Edgar will ask us to remember in the next scene but one,

> the mind much sufferance doth o'erskip,
> When grief hath mates, and bearing fellowship.

VI

Questions like these point ultimately to larger and more abstract questions, over which the action of the play, like Hamlet's melancholy, "sits on brood." One of these has to do with the moral foundations of society. To what extent have our distinctions of degree and status, our regulations by law and usage, moral significance? To what extent are they simply the expedient disguises of a war of all on all, wherein humanity preys on itself (as Albany says) "Like monsters of the deep"? This anxiety, though it permeates the play, is pressed with particular force in the utterances of the mad king to Gloucester in the fields near Dover. Here, as so often in Shakespeare, we encounter an occasion when the barriers between fiction and reality are suddenly collapsed, and the Elizabethan audience was made to realize, as we are, that it was listening to an indictment far more relevant to its own social experience than to any this king of ancient Britain could be imagined to have had. Furthermore, here onstage, as during the scene on the heath, a familiar convention was again being turned upside down and made electric with meaning. A king of the realm — like their own king, guarantee of its coinage ("they cannot touch me for coining"), commander of its troops ("There's your press money"), chief object of its *paideia* ("They flattered me like a dog"), fountain of its justice ("I pardon that man's life"), center of its reverence ("O! let me kiss that hand") — was not only presented mad, crowned with weeds, but in his madness registered for all to hear the bankruptcy of the very body politic (and body moral) of which he was representative and head:

> Plate sin with gold,
> And the strong lance of justice hurtless breaks;
> Arm it in rags, a pigmy's straw does pierce it.
> None does offend, none, I say none; I'll able 'em:
> Take that of me, my friend, who have the power
> To seal th' accuser's lips. Get thee glass eyes;
> And, like a scurvy politician, seem
> To see the things thou dost not.

No one, I suspect, who had responded to the role of the king in Shakespeare's history plays, or the king's role in contemporary drama generally, could miss the shock in these lines, coming as they did from "the thing itself." If we suppose, further, that the structural conventions of the Elizabethan theatre, with its "very solid three-dimensional symbols of order" representing "home, city, and king,"[18]

---

[18] G. R. Kernodle, "The Open Stage: Elizabethan or Existentialist," *Shakespeare Survey*, XII (1959), 3.

sometimes induced in observers a deeper identification, a sense that they were witnessing in the career of the stage monarch a "sacred combat" or ritual struggle that enacted the corporate (and individual) quest for well-being and self-knowledge in the person of the king, we may guess that the shock of this reversal was profound indeed. But we need not suppose so much. Even the most casual playgoer, who had looked about him reflectively in Jacobean England, must have experienced a shudder of self-recognition as Lear's "sermon" proceeded. The gulf between medieval social ideals and contemporary actualities was imposing by Shakespeare's time a significant strain on sensitive minds, the kind of strain that (in a way we are painfully familiar with in our own age) can madden men, as in a sense it has maddened Lear. "The ideal was still Christian," writes Crane Brinton, who has put the matter as pithily as anyone, "still an ideal of unity, peace, security, organization, status; the reality was endemic war, divided authority even at the top, [and] a great scramble for wealth and position." [19]

Lear's vision of society in Dover fields is a vision of this gulf. To a limited extent it relates to his own sufferings, but principally to the society for which it was written, and, I would wish to add, to all societies as such. Under the masks of discipline, Lear's speeches imply, in any imaginable society on earth, there will always lurk the lust of the simpering dame, the insolence of the dog in office, the hypocrisy of the usurer who hangs the cozener, the mad injustice of sane men's choices, like Lear's in disowning Cordelia. Institutions are necessary if society is to exist at all; but as the play here eloquently points out, and as Lear from this point on him-

[19] *Ideas and Men* (1950), p. 269.

self knows, they are not enough.[20] What human relatedness truly means, stripped of its robes and furr'd gowns and all marks of status and images of authority, we are shown in the ensuing scenes of mutual humility and compassion between Lear and Cordelia, Edgar and Gloucester.

A second question that the play keeps bringing before our imaginations in its social dimension is the problem of human identity. It sees this, in part, as a function of status, and it is doubtless not without meaning that so many of the play's persons undergo drastic alterations in the "statistical" sphere. Cordelia is deprived of her place in state and family; Kent, of his earldom; Edgar, of his sonship and patrimony; Gloucester, of his title and lands; Lear, of the whole fabric of familiar relations by which he has always known himself to be Lear and through the loss of which he falls into madness. Yet the matter is also presented to us at a deeper level than that of status. When, at Goneril's Lear cries out, "This is not Lear. . . . Who is it that can tell me who I am?" or, on the heath, staring at Edgar's nakedness, "Is man no more than this?" we realize that his questionings cast a shadow well beyond the limits of the immediate situation as he understands it, a shadow that involves the problem of human identity in its ultimate sense, which has lost none of its agonizing ambiguity with the passage of three centuries. *Is* man, in fact, no more than "this"? — a poor bare forked animal in the wind and rain — or is man a metaphysical conception, a normative term, which suffers violence whenever any human being has been reduced to the condition of "bare fork'd animal," whenever "man's life is cheap as beast's" because the "need" has been too much "reasoned," whenever "man's

---

[20] See particularly on this point Arthur Sewell, *Character and Society in Shakespeare* (1951), pp. 110 ff.

work" (as with Edmund's officer) excludes drawing a cart or eating dried oats but not the murder of his own kind? As the waters rise against our foothold on the cliff of chalk, this has become our question too.

VII

The ultimate uncertainty in *King Lear* to which all others point is, as always in tragedy, the question of man's fate. With its strong emphasis on inexorable and unimaginable consequences unwinding to make a web to which every free and willful act contributes another toil, *King Lear* may claim a place near the absolute center, "the true blank" (so Kent might call it), of tragic experience. "The tragedy of Adam," writes Northrop Frye, following Milton in tracing "the archetypal human tragedy" in the narrative of Genesis, "resolves, like all other tragedies, in the manifestation of natural law. He enters a world in which existence is itself tragic, not existence modified by an act, deliberate or unconscious."[21] This is the form of tragedy I think we all sense at the basis of *King Lear*, and the reason why its windows opening on the pilgrimage and *psychomachia* of a king who is also Rex Humanitas are so relevant to its theme. Existence is tragic in *King Lear* because existence is inseparable from relation; we are born from and to it; it envelops us in our loves and lives as parents, children, sisters, brothers, husbands, wives, servants, masters, rulers, subjects — the web is seamless and unending. When we talk of virtue, patience, courage, joy, we talk of what supports it. When we talk of tyranny, lust, and treason, we talk of what destroys it. There is no human action, Shakespeare shows us,

---

[21] *Anatomy of Criticism* (1957), pp. 212, 213.

that does not affect it and that it does not affect. Old, we begin our play with the need to impose relation — to divide our kingdom, set our rest on someone's kind nursery, and crawl toward our death. Young, we begin it with the need to respond to relation — to define it, resist it even in order to protect it, honor it, or destroy it. Man's tragic fate, as *King Lear* presents it, comes into being with his entry into relatedness, which is his entry into humanity.

In the play's own terms this fate is perhaps best summarized in the crucial concept of "patience." By the time he meets Gloucester in Dover fields, Lear has begun to learn patience; and patience, as he defines it now, is not at all what he had earlier supposed. He had supposed it was the capacity to bear up under the outrages that occur in a corrupt world to oneself; and so he had cried, when Regan and Goneril joined forces against him, "You heavens, give me that patience, patience I need!" Now, with his experience of the storm behind him, his mind still burning with the lurid vision of a world where "None does offend, none," because all are guilty, he sees further. His subject is not personal suffering in what he here says to Gloucester; his subject is the suffering that is rooted in the very fact of being human, and its best symbol is the birth cry of every infant, as if it knew already that to enter humanity is to be born in pain, to suffer pain, and to cause pain.

> Thou must be patient; we came crying hither:
> Thou know'st the first time that we smell the air
> We waul and cry.

Or as George Gascoigne had put it, giving an old sentiment a new turn in his translation of Innocent III's *De Contemptu Mundi*: "We are all borne crying that we may thereby expresse our misery; for a male childe lately borne pronounceth

A [for Adam] and a woman childe pronounceth E [for Eve]:
So that they say eyther E or A: as many as discend from
Eva. . . . Eche of these soundes is the voyce of a sorrowful
creature, expressing the greatnesse of his grefe." [22]

Lear's words to Gloucester, I take it, describe this ultimate
dimension of patience, in which the play invites us to share
at its close. It is the patience to accept the condition of being
human in a scheme of things where the thunder will not
peace at our bidding; where nothing can stay the unfolding
consequences of a rash act, including the rash acts of bearing
and being born;

> where the worst is not
> So long as we can say 'This is the worst';

yet where the capacity to grow and ripen — in relation and
in love — is in some mysterious way bound up with the
capacity to lose, and to suffer, and to endure:

> Men must endure
> Their going hence, even as their coming hither:
> Ripeness is all.

From one half of this tragic knowledge, Lear subsequently
wavers — as Gloucester wavers from what Edgar thought he
had learned at Dover Cliff. Lear would need no crumbs of
comfort after the battle if his sufferings could at last be
counted on to bring rewards — if, for example, he could pass
his declining years in peace and happiness with Cordelia. He
wants to believe that this is possible. He has made the choice
that he should have made in the beginning. He has allied
himself with those who in the world's sense are fools; and
he is prepared to accept the alienation from the world that

---

[22] *Complete Works*, ed. J. W. Cunliffe (1910), II, 220.

this requires, as the famous passage at the opening of the last scene shows. In this passage he puts aside Goneril and Regan forever; he does not even want to see them. He accepts eagerly the prison which marks his withdrawal from the world's values, for he has his own new values to sustain:

> We two alone will sing like birds i' th' cage:
> When thou dost ask me blessing, I'll kneel down
> And ask of thee forgiveness: so we'll live,
> And pray, and sing, and tell old tales, and laugh
> At gilded butterflies, and hear poor rogues
> Talk of court news; and we'll talk with them too,
> Who loses and who wins, who's in, who's out:
> And take upon 's the mystery of things
> As if we were God's spies.

They will be in the world, but not of it. On this kind of sacrifice, he adds, "the Gods themselves throw incense."

But to speak so is to speak from a knowledge that no human experience teaches. If it could end like this, if there were guaranteed rewards like this for making our difficult choices, the play would be a melodrama, and our world very different from what it is. So far as human wisdom goes, the choice of relatedness must be recognized as its own reward, leading sometimes to alleviation of suffering, as in the case of Gloucester's joy in Edgar, but equally often to more suffering, as in the case of Lear. For Lear, like many another, has to make the difficult choice only to lose the fruits of it. Not in his own death — as Kent says, "he hates him That would upon the rack of this tough world Stretch him out longer" — but in Cordelia's. Cordelia, our highest choice, is what we always want the gods to guarantee. But to this the gods will not consent. Hence when Albany exclaims, at Edmund's confession that he has ordered Cordelia's death, "The gods defend her," the gods' answer to that is, as Bradley pointed out long ago, "Enter Lear, with Cordelia in his arms." [23]

In his last speech, the full implications of the human condition evidently come home to Lear. He has made his choice, and there will be no reward. Again and again, in his repetitions, he seems to be trying to drive this final tragic fact into his human consciousness, where it never wants to stick:

> No, no, no life!
> Why should a dog, a horse, a rat have life
> And thou no breath at all? Thou'lt come no more,
> Never, never, never, never, never!

He tries to hold this painful vision unflinchingly before his consciousness, but the strain, considering everything else he has been through, is too great: consciousness itself starts to give way: "Pray you, undo this button: thank you, Sir." And with it the vision gives way too: he cannot sustain it; he dies, reviving in his heart the hope that Cordelia lives: "Look on her, look, her lips, Look there, look there!"

VIII

We are offered two ways of being sentimental about this conclusion, both of which we must make an effort to eschew. One is to follow those who argue that, because these last lines probably mean that Lear dies in the joy of thinking Cordelia lives, some sort of mitigation or transfiguration has been reached which turns defeat into total victory. "Only to earthbound intelligence," says Professor O. J. Campbell, "is Lear pathetically deceived in thinking Cordelia alive. Those familiar with the Morality

---

[23] *Op. cit.*, p. 326.

plays will realize that Lear has found in her unselfish love the one companion who is willing to go with him through Death up to the throne of the Everlasting Judge." [24] I think most of us will agree that this is too simple. Though there is much of the Morality play in *Lear*, it is not used toward a morality theme, but, as I have tried to suggest in this essay, toward building a deeply metaphysical metaphor, or myth, about the human condition, the state of man, in which the last of many mysteries is the enigmatic system of relatedness in which he is enclosed.

The other sentimentality leads us to indulge the currently fashionable existentialist *nausée*, and to derive from the fact that Lear's joy is mistaken, or, alternatively, from the fact that in the Lear world "even those who have fully repented, done penance, and risen to the tender regard of sainthood can be hunted down, driven insane, and killed by the most agonizing extremes of passion," [25] the conclusion that "we inhabit an imbecile universe." [26] Perhaps we do — but Shakespeare's *King Lear* provides no evidence of it that till now we lacked. That love, compassion, hope, and truth are "subjects all," not only to "envious and calumniating time," but to purest casualty and mischance has been the lament of poets since Homer. Shakespeare can hardly have imagined that in *King Lear*'s last scene he was telling his audiences something they had never known, or was casting his solemn vote on one side or other of the vexing philosophical and theological questions involved in the suffering of the innocent and good. The scene has, besides, his characteristic ambiguity and balance. No world beyond this one in which "all manner of things will be

---

[24] "The Salvation of Lear," *ELH*, XV (1948), 107.

[25] J. Stampfer, "The Catharsis of *King Lear*," *Shakespeare Survey*, XIII (1960), 4.

[26] *Ibid.*, p. 10.

well" is asserted; but neither is it denied: Kent happens to take it for granted and will follow his master beyond that horizon as he has beyond every other: "My master calls me, I must not say no." Edgar has come to soberer assessments of reality than he was given to making in the forepart of the play, but his instinctive kindness (we may assume) is unabated and has survived all trials. Lear's joy in thinking that his daughter lives (if this is what his words imply) is illusory, but it is one we need not begrudge him on his deathbed, as we do not begrudge it to a dying man in hospital whose family has just been wiped out. Nor need we draw elaborate inferences from its illusoriness about the imbecility of our world; in a similar instance among our acquaintances, we would regard the illusion as a godsend, or even, if we were believers, as God-sent.

In short, to say, with an increasing number of recent critics, that "the remorseless process of *King Lear*" forces us to "face the fact of its ending without any support from systems of moral . . . belief at all"[27] is to indulge the mid-twentieth-century *frisson du néant* at its most sentimental. We face the ending of this play, as we face our world, with whatever support we customarily derive from systems of belief or unbelief. If the sound of David crying "Absalom, my son," the image of Mary bending over another broken child, the motionless form of a missionary doctor whose martyrdom is recent, not to mention all that earth has known of disease, famine, earthquake, war, and prison since men first came crying hither — if our moral and religious systems can survive this, and the record suggests that for many good men they do and can, then clearly they will have no trouble in surviv-

---

[27] Nicholas Brooke, *Shakespeare: King Lear* (1963), p. 60.

ing the figure of Lear as he bends in his agony, or in his joy, above Cordelia. Tragedy never tells us what to think; it shows us what we are and may be. And what we are and may be was never, I submit, more memorably fixed upon a stage than in this kneeling old man whose heartbreak is precisely the measure of what, in our world of relatedness, it is possible to lose and possible to win. The victory and the defeat are simultaneous and inseparable.

If there is any "remorseless process" in *King Lear*, it is one that begs us to seek the meaning of our human fate not in what becomes of us, but in what we become. Death, as we saw, is miscellaneous and commonplace; it is life whose quality may be made noble and distinctive. Suffering we all recoil from; but we know it is a greater thing to suffer than to lack the feelings and virtues that make it possible to suffer. Cordelia, we may choose to say, accomplished nothing, yet we know it is better to have been Cordelia than to have been her sisters. When we come crying hither, we bring with us the badge of all our misery; but it is also the badge of the vulnerabilities that give us access to whatever grandeur we achieve.

Index

Index

Index

Index

Index

Index

Richard II, theme of substance vs. shadow, 51
Romeo and Juliet, contrasted with *KL*, 5, 85